12

D1123674

SPOTLIGHT ON LITERACY

Authors, Consultants, and Reviewers

MULTICULTURAL AND EDUCATIONAL
CONSULTANTS

Alma Flor Ada, Yvonne Beamer, Joyce Buckner,
Helen Gillotte, Cheryl Hudson, Narcita Medina,
Lorraine Monroe, James R. Murphy, Sylvia Peña,
Joseph B. Rubin, Ramon Santiago, Cliff Trafzer,
Hai Tran, Esther Lee Yao

LITERATURE CONSULTANTS

Ashley Bryan, Joan I. Glazer, Paul Janeczko,
Margaret H. Lippert

INTERNATIONAL CONSULTANTS

Edward B. Adams, Barbara Johnson,
Raymond L. Marshall

MUSIC AND AUDIO CONSULTANTS

John Farrell, Marilyn C. Davidson,
Vincent Lawrence, Sarah Pirtle, Susan R. Synder,
Rick and Deborah Witkowski, Eastern Sky Media
Services, Inc.

TEACHER REVIEWERS

Terry Baker, Jane Bauer, James Bedi, Nora Bickel,
Vernell Bowen, Donald Cason, Jean Chaney,
Carolyn Clark, Alan Cox, Kathryn DesCarpentrie,
Carol L. Ellis, Roberta Gale, Brenda Huffman,
Erma Inscore, Sharon Kidwell, Elizabeth Love,
Isabel Marcus, Elaine McCraney, Michelle Moraros,
Earlene Parr, Dr. Richard Potts, Jeanette Pulliam,
Michael Rubin, Henrietta Sakamaki,
Kathleen Cultron Sanders, Belinda Snow,
Dr. Jayne Steubing, Margaret Mary Sulentic,
Barbara Tate, Seretta Vincent,
Willard Waite, Barbara Wilson, Veronica York

Macmillan/McGraw-Hill

A Division of The McGraw-Hill Companies

Copyright © 1997 Macmillan/McGraw-Hill,
a Division of the Educational and Professional
Publishing Group of The McGraw-Hill Companies, Inc.

Macmillan/McGraw-Hill
1221 Avenue of the Americas
New York, New York 10020

Printed in the United States of America

ISBN 0-02-181005-2 / 2, L.6
8 9 V H J 02 01 00

Spotlight on Literacy

AUTHORS

ELAINE MEI AOKI • VIRGINIA ARNOLD • JAMES FLOOD • JAMES V. HOFFMAN • DIANE LAPP

MIRIAM MARTINEZ • ANNEMARIE SULLIVAN PALINCSAR • MICHAEL PRIESTLEY • CARL B. SMITH

WILLIAM H. TEALE • JOSEFINA VILLAMIL TINAJERO • ARNOLD W. WEBB • KAREN D. WOOD

Macmillan McGraw-Hill

NEW YORK • FARMINGTON

Unit 1

FAMILY FUN

Unit 2

EUREKA!

7

Unit 3

BETTER TOGETHER

Unit 1

Charlie Anderson

by Barbara Abercrombie
illustrated by Mark Graham

One cold night a cat walked out of the woods, up the steps, across the deck, and into the house where Elizabeth and Sarah lived.

He curled up next to their fireplace to get warm.
He watched the six o'clock news on TV.

He tasted their dinner. He tried out their beds.

He decided to stay, and the girls named him
Charlie. Every morning Charlie disappeared into the
woods again.

At night when he came home, Elizabeth brushed
him clean, fed him dinner, and made a space for him
at the foot of her bed.

He liked Elizabeth's bed the best. Sometimes she would wake up in the middle of the night and hear him purring in the dark.

Sarah called him Baby and dressed him up in doll clothes.

When it snowed, Elizabeth and Sarah's mother heated Charlie's milk before he left for the woods.

He grew fatter and fatter, and every day he purred louder and louder.

On weekends the girls stayed with their father and stepmother in the city. They wanted to bring Charlie with them, but their mother said he'd miss the woods. "Charlie's a country cat," she told them.

One stormy night Charlie didn't come home. Elizabeth and Sarah stayed out on the deck and called and called his name. But no Charlie.

Where was he? Why wouldn't he come out of the woods? Was he all right?

All night long Elizabeth listened to the rain beating on the roof and the wind rattling the windows. Was he cold? Was he hurt? Where was Charlie?

In the morning Elizabeth and Sarah looked for him. They asked the lady down the road if she'd seen their cat. She said no, and offered them cookies. But they were too worried to eat anything, even her chocolate-chip cookies.

They went to the new house on the other side
of the woods. "Have you seen our cat?" they asked.
"His name is Charlie. He's very fat and has gray
striped fur."

"We have a cat with gray striped fur," said the
man. "But his name's not Charlie, it's Anderson. He's
upstairs, asleep on our bed."

They heard a meow, and down the stairs came a very fat cat with gray striped fur. "Charlie!" Sarah and Elizabeth cried.

"No, that's Anderson," said the woman. "We've had him for seven years. Right, Anderson?"

He looked at her and began to purr.

"But it's *Charlie*," Sarah said.

He looked at her and purred louder.

"Is he ever here at night?" Elizabeth asked.

"Anderson is a hunter," said the man. "He prowls the woods at night."

"Charlie sleeps in my bed at night," Elizabeth said. "He leaves for the woods after breakfast."

"Anderson comes home at breakfast time," said the woman. "He leaves right after dinner." They all looked at the cat. He sat at their feet, very happy and very fat.

They call him Charlie Anderson now.

Sometimes, in bed at night, Elizabeth asks him, "Who do you love best, Charlie Anderson?" And she can hear him purring in the dark.

Just like Elizabeth and Sarah, Charlie has two houses, two beds, two families who love him.

He's a lucky cat.

MEET
Barbara Abercrombie

Barbara Abercrombie writes books for children and adults. She has always enjoyed telling stories. She says, "When I was a little girl, my favorite pastime was making up stories for paper dolls." She likes to act, but writing is most important to her. "I like writing for both children and adults. I find that the stories all come from the same place—trying to make sense of life," she says.

MEET
Mark Graham

Mark Graham was born in Salt Lake City, Utah. He went to New York when he was young to study art. Many people across the United States have seen his paintings in art shows. He has also illustrated several books for children. They include picture books and a biography. When he paints, he tries to use light to make his pictures more interesting. He often uses his three sons as models for his pictures.

October Saturday

by Bobbi Katz

All the leaves have turned to cornflakes.
It looks as if some giant's baby brother
had tipped the box
and scattered them upon our lawn—
millions and millions of cornflakes—
crunching, crunching under our feet.
When the wind blows,
they rattle against each other,
nervously chattering.

We rake them into piles—
Dad and I.
Piles and piles of cornflakes!
A breakfast for a whole family of giants!
We do not talk much as we rake—
a word here—
a word there.
The leaves are never silent.

Inside the house my mother is packing
short sleeved shirts and faded bathing suits—
rubber clogs and flippers—
in a box marked SUMMER.

We are raking,
Dad and I.
Raking, raking.
The sky is blue, then orange, then gray.
My arms are tired.
I am dreaming of the box marked SUMMER.

Meet Cynthia Rylant

Cynthia Rylant says, "The idea for Henry and Mudge came from my own life. I once owned a 200-pound English mastiff named Mudge. My son, Nate, was seven years old at the time. The two together became Henry and Mudge in my books.

"Anyone who's ever loved a dog knows what a treasure a good dog is. You just can't be unhappy for very long when you have a good dog licking your face, shaking your hand, and drooling all over your shoes."

Meet Suçie Stevenson

Suçie Stevenson loves to draw pictures for the stories about Henry and Mudge. She says: "The stories are about things that have happened to me."

When asked if she had anything to tell children who might like to be artists, Ms. Stevenson said: "Don't listen to what others tell you to draw. Put colors where you want them. Just start drawing."

Henry and Mudge

Story by Cynthia Rylant
Pictures by Suçie Stevenson

Henry

Henry had no brothers
and no sisters.
"I want a brother,"
he told his parents.
"Sorry," they said.
Henry had no friends
on his street.

"I want to live
on a different street,"
he told his parents.
"Sorry," they said.
Henry had no pets
at home.
"I want to have a dog,"
he told his parents.
"Sorry," they *almost* said.

But first they looked
at their house
with no brothers and sisters.
Then they looked
at their street
with no children.
Then they looked
at Henry's face.

Then they looked at each other.
"Okay," they said.
"I want to hug you!"
Henry told his parents.
And he did.

Mudge

Henry searched for a dog.

"Not just any dog," said Henry.

"Not a short one," he said.

"Not a curly one," he said.

"And no pointed ears."

Then he found Mudge.
Mudge had floppy ears,
not pointed.
And Mudge had straight fur,
not curly.
But Mudge was short.
"Because he's a puppy,"
Henry said.
"He'll grow."

And did he ever!

He grew out of his puppy cage.

He grew out of his dog cage.

He grew out of seven collars
in a row.

And when he finally
stopped growing . . .

he weighed one hundred eighty pounds,
he stood three feet tall,
and he drooled.
"I'm glad you're not short,"
Henry said.

And Mudge licked him,
then sat on him.

HeNry

Henry used to walk
to school alone.
When he walked
he used to worry about
tornadoes,
ghosts,
biting dogs,
and bullies.

He walked as fast
as he could.
He looked straight ahead.
He never looked back.
But now he walked to school
with Mudge.

And now when he walked,
he thought about
vanilla ice cream,
rain,
rocks,
and good dreams.
He walked to school
but not too fast.
He walked to school
and sometimes backward.

He walked to school
and patted Mudge's big head,
happy.

Adopting ❀ Daisy

Art by Mike Eagle

The Orejas family has decided they want to adopt a pet. They are coming to the animal shelter to find one. All of these animals need good homes.

Mike likes a beautiful big dog. Rusty's owner moved away and could not take him along. Rusty needs a big fenced yard to run in. The Orejas family lives in an apartment. "Let's look for a cat," says Mrs. Orejas.

Mimi finds a mother cat with seven tiny, fuzzy kittens. How cute they are! But they are too little to leave their mother.

Then Mike sees Daisy. Someone found Daisy in the street and brought her here. She was hungry and scared at first, but now she is healthy and safe.

Daisy wants to play with Mimi's braids. Mimi giggles, "Look, she likes me!"

Mike rolls a ball, and Daisy pounces on it. She is frisky and playful. But when Mimi picks her up, she is gentle, too.

"She's cute!" says Mike. "Let's take her home," says Mimi.

55

Mr. and Mrs. Orejas pay a small adoption fee and sign an agreement to take good care of Daisy for the rest of her life. Mimi and Mike promise to help.

The veterinarian gives Daisy shots to protect her from getting sick. She gives Mimi a little book about cat care.

At her new house, Daisy will have her own cat bed and food dish and water bowl. She will have a scratching post and a litter box, too.

Mike and Mimi can't wait to show Daisy her new home.

EVERYBODY SAYS

Everybody says
I look just like my mother.
Everybody says
I'm the image of Aunt Bee.
Everybody says
My nose is like my father's,
But *I* want to look like *me*.

Dorothy Aldis

ANDRE

I had a dream last night. I dreamed
I had to pick a Mother out.
I had to choose a Father too.
At first, I wondered what to do,
There were so many there, it seemed,
Short and tall and thin and stout.

But just before I sprang awake,
I knew what parents I would take.

And *this* surprised and made me glad:
They were the ones I always had!

GWENDOLYN BROOKS

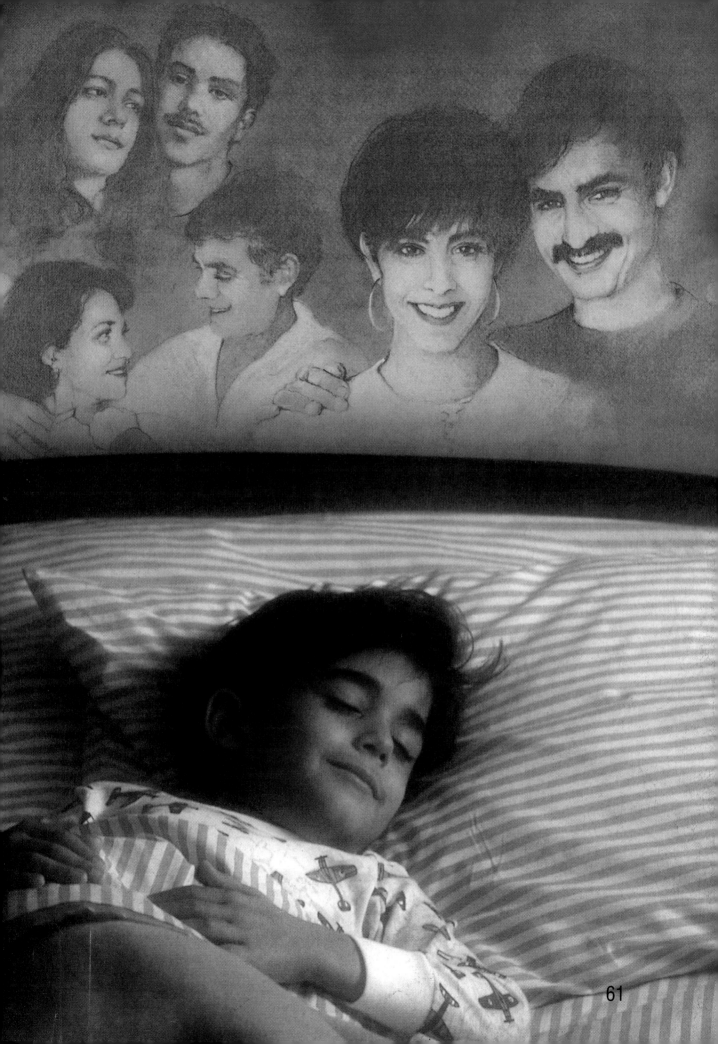

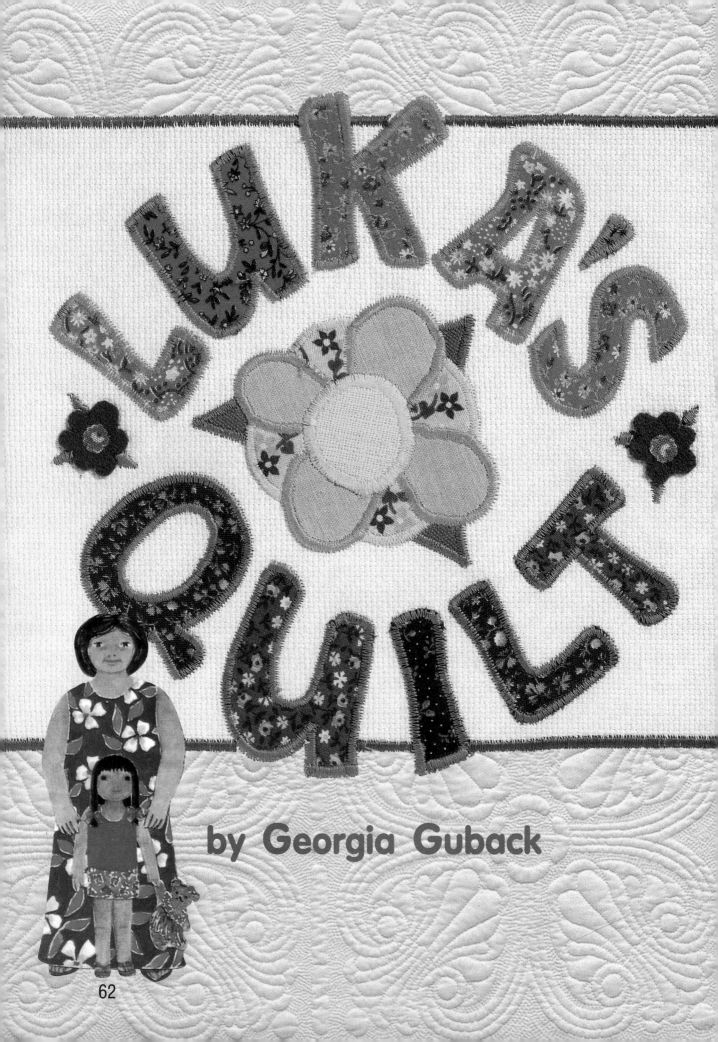

LUKA'S QUILT

by Georgia Guback

My tutu lives with us. Tutu. That's Hawaiian for grandmother. Tutu takes care of me while Mom and Dad work. We do lots of things together. I like that, and so does Tutu. But all that changed when the quilt came along.

One morning Tutu said, "I had a dream last night. I dreamed I was in a beautiful garden. There were flowers everywhere. It gave me an idea for a quilt. This quilt will be for you, Luka. I made a quilt for your mom. Now it's your turn."

"Will it have flowers on it?" I asked.

"Oh yes," Tutu replied. "It's a flower garden. There will be all kinds of flowers."

"It's going to be so pretty," I said.

"It will take a long time to make," said Tutu. "You'll have to be patient."

"That's okay," I said. "I can help."

After breakfast Tutu and I went to the fabric store.

"Choose a color," said Tutu.

There were so many pretty colors.

"I like that yellow," I said. "And that pink. And some of that blue. And the lavender. And this orange is nice."

Tutu laughed. "Not so fast," she said. "Choose one color. Just one."

"How can it be a flower garden if there's just one color?" I asked.

"You'll see," said Tutu.

Just one color! Green. I chose green because flowers have green leaves. The flower colors would come later.

Tutu sketched and cut and pinned and basted. And I got to help. This quilt is going to be so pretty, I kept thinking. I could hardly wait for the flowers.

At last Tutu put the quilt on the quilting frame. "Serious work now," she said. And I knew I wasn't big enough to help anymore.

"When are the flowers coming, Tutu?" I'd ask.

She'd smile and answer, "You'll see, Luka. You'll see."

Then one day a long time after, Tutu took the quilt off the frame. She ironed it and put it on my bed. "For you, Luka," she said.

The flowers! There were no flowers! "Where are the flowers?" I cried.

"Here," said Tutu. "See, here's amaryllis. And here's ginger. And over there is jacaranda."

"Everything's white," I said. "How can there be flowers with no pretty flower colors?"

"This is the way we make our quilts," said Tutu. "Two colors. It's our Island tradition. You chose green, remember?"

"I thought the green was for leaves," I cried. "All the flowers in our garden are in colors. It can't be a flower garden if the flowers are white."

Tutu's eyes got watery, and she quietly turned and went to her room and shut the door.

I looked at Tutu's quilt again. I thought it was going to be so pretty, and all it was was white.

I sat down and cried.

Things changed after that. Tutu and I used to be such good friends. Now we had nothing to say to each other. We didn't do things together anymore. And all because of that quilt. It's going to stay like this forever, I thought. It was awful.

But Tutu surprised me. A few days later she said, "Today is Lei Day. You've never been to a Lei Day celebration, Luka. Let's declare a truce and see what's going on at the park."

"What's a truce?" I asked.

"That's when people put aside their differences and come together again for a little while," Tutu answered.

I didn't see how that was going to work, but it was worth a try.

"Okay," I said.

I filled the water jug, and Tutu got the tatami mat, and we stopped at Aiko's to buy bento for our picnic. By the time the bus came, it was almost beginning to feel like old times.

There was so much going on at the park. We listened to the music. We watched the dancing. We spread our mat under a tree and ate our bento. And Tutu treated me to shave ice.

Later we came to a place where kids were making leis.

"Come," said a lady. "Make a lei."

"Is it okay, Tutu?" I asked.

"Go ahead," said Tutu.

The lady got me started. She gave me a long needle and strong thread and showed me how to string the flowers together.

There were all kinds of blossoms. They were in cardboard boxes with wet newspapers all around to keep them fresh. I chose a pink flower. Next I added a yellow. Then an orange. And then a lavender. Tutu laughed. "No, not that way, Luka," she said. "Choose one color, maybe two. But no more than two."

I could feel myself getting angry, and I tried not to. I was remembering our truce.

"Tutu," I said, "it's my lei."

"But . . . ," Tutu began. Then she stopped. She was remembering our truce, too, and she didn't say another word.

Things got better at once. I didn't feel angry anymore, and I made my lei my way. It turned out very pretty, and I got to keep it and wear it home.

So the truce worked, and I felt happy. "I'm glad you had that truce idea, Tutu," I said. "I had a good time."

"So did I," Tutu answered.

By bedtime the happy feeling was still with me. I looked at Tutu's quilt again. Maybe a white flower garden wasn't so bad. I snuggled underneath her quilt and fell asleep.

The next day Tutu said, "Luka, I was looking at your lei last night. I saw your flower garden in it, and it gave me an idea."

I got to help with Tutu's idea. I chose pretty flower colors from her scrap baskets, and then I helped sketch and cut and baste. Then Tutu did the sewing and quilting.

A long time later, after my pretty flower lei had dried out and turned brown, Tutu called me. We went to my bedroom. And there they were—like magic! All the flowers I had dreamed of in a special quilted lei!

"Just for you, Luka," said Tutu. "Now you have all your flowers and all your colors."

"Oh, it's so pretty!" I cried.

And all at once I was hugging Tutu and she was hugging me back. And everything was better again.

I like my quilt a lot now. Sometimes I have it plain—
my white flower garden. And sometimes I put Tutu's quilted
lei on top and have my flower garden in color. I like it both
ways. But what I like most is that Tutu and I are friends
again. And I can tell Tutu likes that best of all, too.

MEET
Georgia Guback

Georgia Guback got the idea for *Luka's Quilt* after she saw a Hawaiian quilt. She liked the quilt so much she decided to find out more about Hawaii. She used the facts she learned to write the book.

"I like to communicate with young children. I hope my books help children see that they can find answers to problems," she says. She plans to write many more children's books.

Lei Day:

On May Day, the first of May, lots of people around the world celebrate spring. In Hawaii, they celebrate island-style—May Day is Lei Day! Here are some of the sights, sounds, and smells of Lei Day.

"On Lei Day, I feel happy because I dance and everybody watches the king and queen dance."

Jens Coloma

"String the flowers into a lei,
A delightful lei for Lei Day.
The colours of red and yellow,
To give to a fellow."

Melissa Nii

"Haku leis are braided with two or more materials and flower leis can be sewn with a needle and thread."

Makapuu Awo

"Giving a lei to an older person shows respect."

Mitchell Kululois

"On Lei Day, I smell hot dogs and spam musubi —they smell good!"

Brianne A. Pasion

Party in the Islands!

"The ti leaf lei is worn for protection on adventures in the mountains and the sea."

Hiwa and Devon Baxter

"I celebrate Lei Day by giving leis."

Alexis Marquez, 8

"Kaluhea and I dance hula in front of the queen."

Shantel Wilcox, 8

"Girls and boys go round and round the maypole, making a braid."

Johnette Rittmeister, 8

"I celebrate Lei Day with my two cousins. We dance hula, sing together, and have fun."

Toni Martin, 8

"On Lei Day, the people have a king and queen."

Stasia Chang

Carry Go

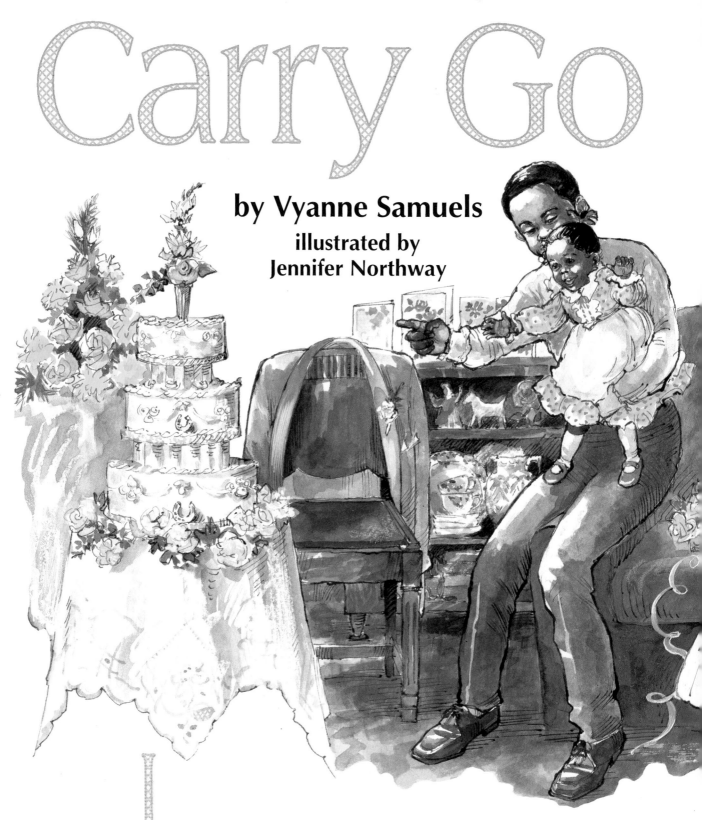

by Vyanne Samuels

illustrated by
Jennifer Northway

It was Saturday morning at Leon's house. It
was a big Saturday morning at Leon's house. It was
Marcia's wedding day. Marcia was Leon's sister.

Bring Come

Everyone in the house was getting
ready for the big Saturday morning.
Everyone was getting ready for the big wedding.

Everyone, that is, except Leon, who was
fast asleep downstairs.

"Wake up, Leon!" shouted his mother upstairs. But Leon did not move.

"Wake up, Leon!" shouted his sister Marlene upstairs.

But Leon did not move.

Leon's mother and his sisters,
Marlene and Marcia, were so busy taking big
blue rollers out of their hair that they forgot to
shout at Leon to wake up again.

They were getting ready for the big day.

They were getting ready for Marcia's wedding.

"Wake up, Leon," said Grandma softly downstairs.

Leon's two eyes opened up immediately.

Leon was awake.

"Carry this up to your mother," said Grandma, handing him a pink silk flower.

Leon ran upstairs to the bedroom with the pink silk flower. But before he could knock on the door, his sister Marcia called to him.

"Wait a little," she said, and she handed him a white veil. "Carry this down to Grandma."

So Leon put the flower between his teeth and the veil in his two hands and ran down the stairs to Grandma.

When he got to his grandma's door,
she called to him before he could knock.
"Wait a little," she said. He waited.

"Carry these up to Marlene," she said,
and she poked a pair of blue shoes out at him.

So Leon put the veil on his head,
kept the flower between his teeth, and
carried the shoes in his two hands.
He tripped upstairs to Marlene.

But when he got to the bedroom door, Marlene called to him before he could knock.

"Wait a little," she said, and she poked a pair of yellow gloves through the door. "Carry these down to Grandma."

S o Leon put the gloves
on his hands,

the shoes on his feet,

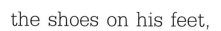

the veil on his head,
and the pink silk flower
between his teeth.

He wobbled downstairs to Grandma, who called to him before he could knock.

"Wait a little," she said. He waited.

"Carry this to Marcia," she said, and she poked a green bottle of perfume through the door.

"Mind how you go," she said.

So Leon climbed the stairs
carefully holding the green bottle of perfume,
carefully wearing the yellow gloves,
carefully dragging the blue shoes,
carefully balancing the white veil,
carefully biting the pink silk flower . . .
when suddenly he could go no further and shouted

"HELP!"

from the middle of the stairs.

He nearly swallowed the flower.

His mother ran out of the room upstairs,
his sister Marlene ran out of the room upstairs,

and Grandma rushed out of her room downstairs.

There was a big silence. They all looked at Leon.

"Look 'pon his feet!" said his mother.

"Look 'pon his fingers and his hands!" said Marlene.

"Look 'pon his head!" said Grandma.

"Look 'pon his mouth!" said Marcia.

And they all let go a big laugh!

Leon looked like a bride!

One by one, Mother, Marcia,
Marlene, and Grandma took away the pink
silk flower, the white veil, the green bottle of
perfume, the blue shoes, and the yellow gloves.

"When am I going to get dressed for the wedding?" asked Leon, wearing just his pajamas now.

"Just wait a little!" said Grandma.

Leon's two eyes opened wide.

"YOU MEAN I HAVE TO WAIT A LITTLE?" he shrieked.

And before anyone could answer, he ran downstairs . . .

and jumped straight back into his bed, without waiting even a little.

Meet Vyanne Samuels

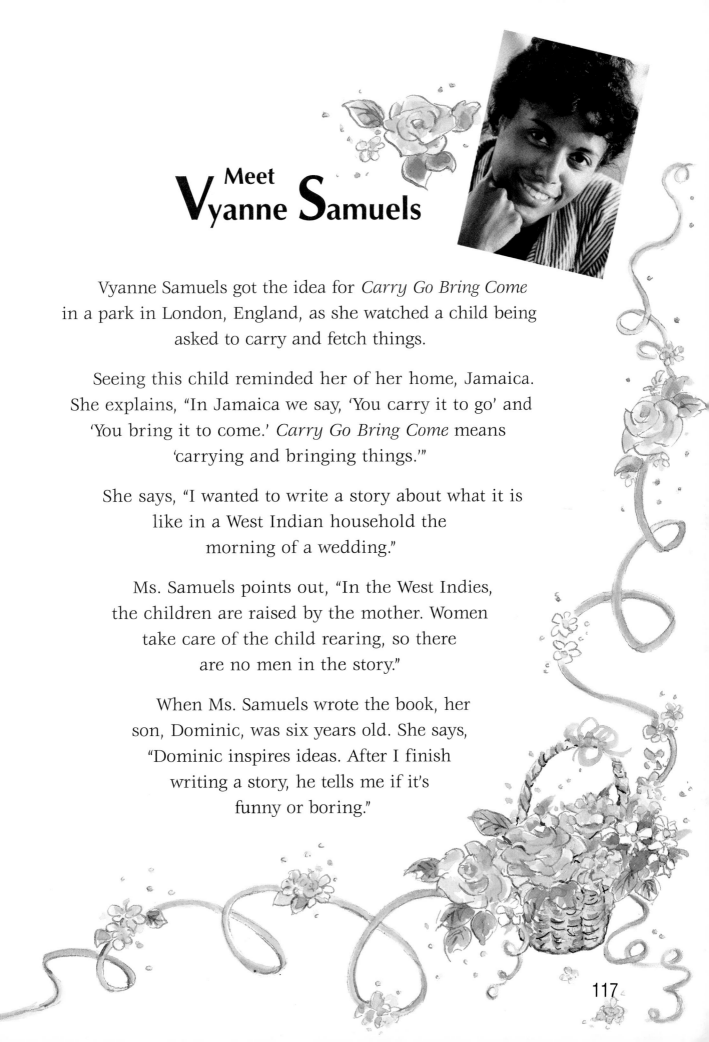

Vyanne Samuels got the idea for *Carry Go Bring Come* in a park in London, England, as she watched a child being asked to carry and fetch things.

Seeing this child reminded her of her home, Jamaica. She explains, "In Jamaica we say, 'You carry it to go' and 'You bring it to come.' *Carry Go Bring Come* means 'carrying and bringing things.'"

She says, "I wanted to write a story about what it is like in a West Indian household the morning of a wedding."

Ms. Samuels points out, "In the West Indies, the children are raised by the mother. Women take care of the child rearing, so there are no men in the story."

When Ms. Samuels wrote the book, her son, Dominic, was six years old. She says, "Dominic inspires ideas. After I finish writing a story, he tells me if it's funny or boring."

117

Dad

mom

Cousins

Brother

Aunt and Uncle

Brownie

118

RELATIVES

BY JEFF MOSS

(A Poem To Say Fast When You Want To Show Off)

My father's and mother's sisters and brothers

Are called my uncles and aunts

(Except when they're called *ma tante* and *mon oncle*

Which happens if they're in France.)

Now the daughters and sons of my uncles and aunts

Are my cousins. (Confusion increases—

Since if you're my mother or if you're my Dad,

Then those cousins are nephews and nieces.)

pictures by Fannellie Ann Ortiz
second grader

119

Unit 2

EUREKA!

THE
SUN
IS ALWAYS
SHINING
SOMEWHERE

by Allan Fowler

The sun is very important to us. You and
I need the sun to grow and be healthy.

Plants need the sun to grow and blossom.

Animals need sunshine, too.

Sunshine makes many good things happen. Tomatoes ripen and so do pumpkins.

Did you know that the sun is a star?

It looks bigger than other stars. But it's not. The sun looks bigger than other stars because it's closer to us than other stars.

Here's one way you can think about why the sun looks bigger than other stars in the sky.

An airplane flying high in the sky looks very small, doesn't it?

But if you've been to the airport and seen an airplane up close, you know that it is really very big. In the same way, the sun looks bigger than other, faraway stars.

The sun never stops shining.

Do you know why you can't see the sun at night?

To find the answer, turn on a lamp in a dark room. Put a tiny mark on a ball. Pretend the mark is you. Imagine the ball is the Earth.

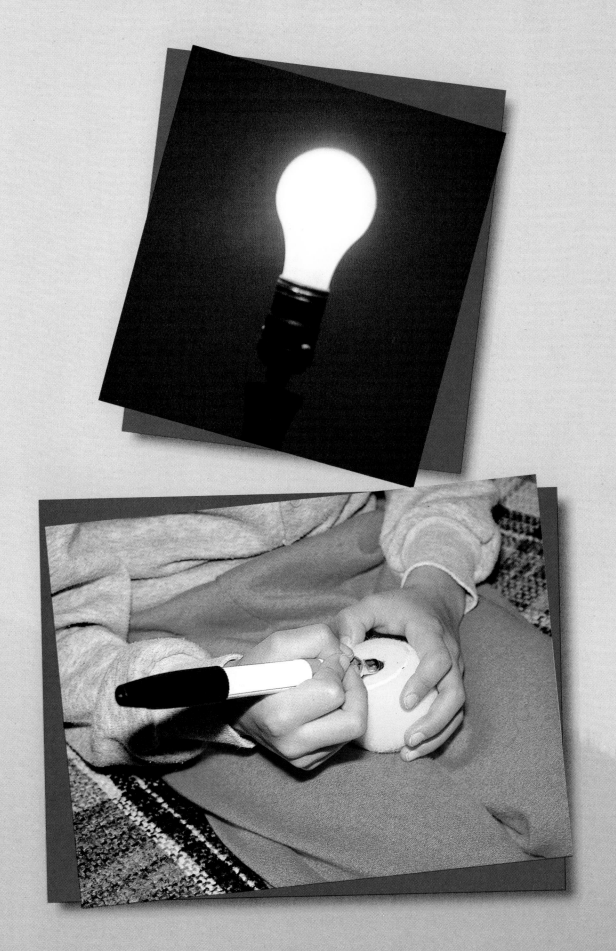

Now hold the ball in front of the lamp. Slowly turn the ball around. The part of it that was lit up by the lamp before is now in the dark. The part that was dark before is now in the light. Earth is like a ball— a very big ball. It is always turning.

It turns out of the sunlight and into the dark of night. Then back into the sunlight the next morning.

Isn't this nice to know?

Even when you're asleep at night, the sun is always shining—somewhere.

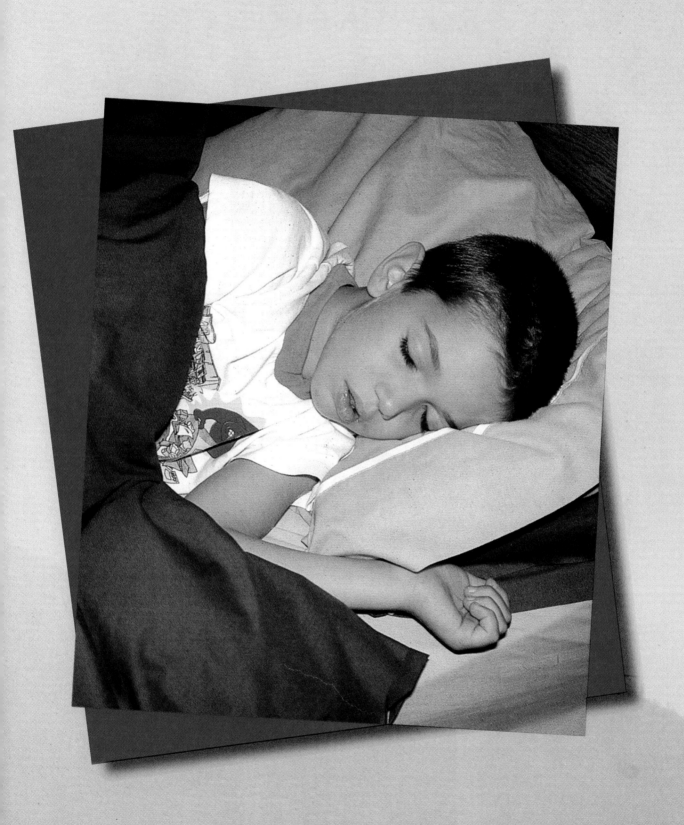

WORDS YOU KNOW

sun

warmth

sunlight

star

Earth

night

morning

MEET
ALLAN FOWLER

Allan Fowler has always been curious about
the world. When he was a boy, he loved to visit
museums and zoos. "I was lucky because we lived
within walking distance of famous museums in
New York City, as well as the Central Park Zoo," he
says. Back then, he could only dream about going
to all the places he saw in pictures and displays.
Today he travels around the world. He has written
over fifty science books for children.

WHAT IS A SHADOW?

by Bob Ridiman • Art by True Kelley

The sun shines *on* you and *around* you but not *through* you. Your body blocks the light and makes your shadow.

In the early morning
and late afternoon,
the sun is low in the
sky. Your shadow is
long and skinny.

Where is the sun
when your shadow
is short and fat?

A shadow tells time on this paper-plate sundial. Push a pencil into the ground through the center of an upside-down paper plate. Every hour, number the pencil's shadow. Don't move your sundial. The next day it will tell you the time.

Shadow animals are fun to make. Here is a bird in flight.

Here is a dog. What other shadow animals can you make?

A SPIKE OF GREEN

When I went out
The sun was hot.
It shone upon
My flower pot.

And there I saw
A spike of green
That no one else
Had ever seen!

On other days
The things I see
Are mostly old
Except for me.

But this green spike
So new and small
Had never yet
Been seen at all!

BARBARA BAKER

149

Meet
Joyce Durham Barrett

"The idea for *Willie's Not the Hugging Kind* came from two boys I knew—Willie and Anthony," explains Joyce Durham Barrett. "On the way home from the library, I stopped by to visit my sister, and I was hugging everyone there. When I got to my nephew, Anthony, he jumped up saying, 'No, no! I'm not the hugging kind!' Anthony's words got mixed up with the boy Willie, and that's how I came up with the story."

Meet
Pat Cummings

Pat Cummings used people she knew as models for the illustrations in *Willie's Not the Hugging Kind.* "Knowing and caring about the models helps me to show the warmth and caring of the family in the story."

When asked how she drew the pictures for this book, Pat Cummings said, "The first thing I did was think about what pictures I wanted to illustrate. Then I made sketches of what I wanted to show. Then I had the models pose for me like the sketches, and I took photographs of the models. Later on I drew the illustrations."

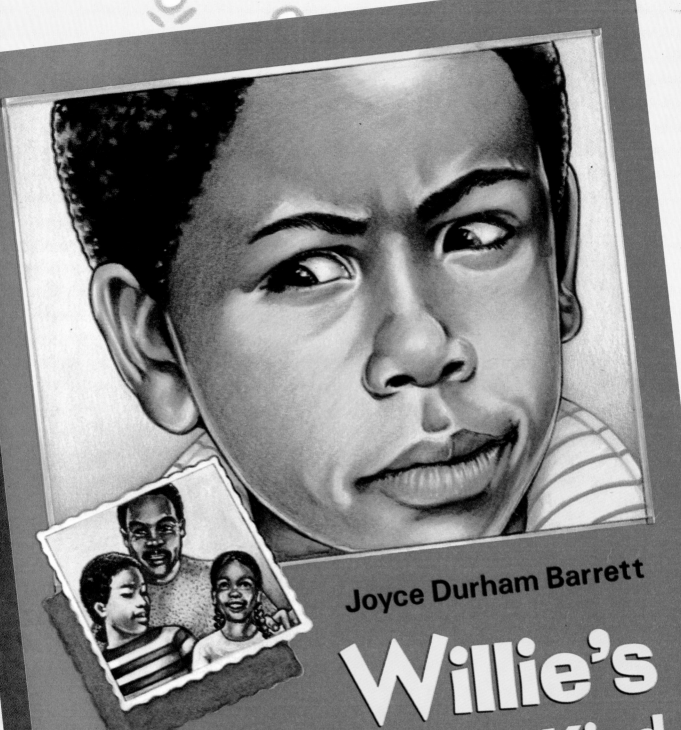

Joyce Durham Barrett

Willie's
Not the Hugging Kind

illustrated by Pat Cummings

Willie wanted someone to hug. That's what he wanted more than anything.

But no one hugged Willie. Not anymore.

Not even his daddy when he dropped Willie and his friend Jo-Jo off at school. Now, he just patted Willie on the head and said, "See you around, Son."

Willie didn't like to be patted on the head. It made him feel like a little dog. Besides, hugging felt much nicer, no matter what Jo-Jo said.

Every day Jo-Jo rode to school in the linen truck with Willie and his daddy. And when Willie used to hug his daddy good-bye, Jo-Jo would turn his head and laugh. "What did you do that for? Man, that's silly," Jo-Jo would say once they had crawled out of the truck.

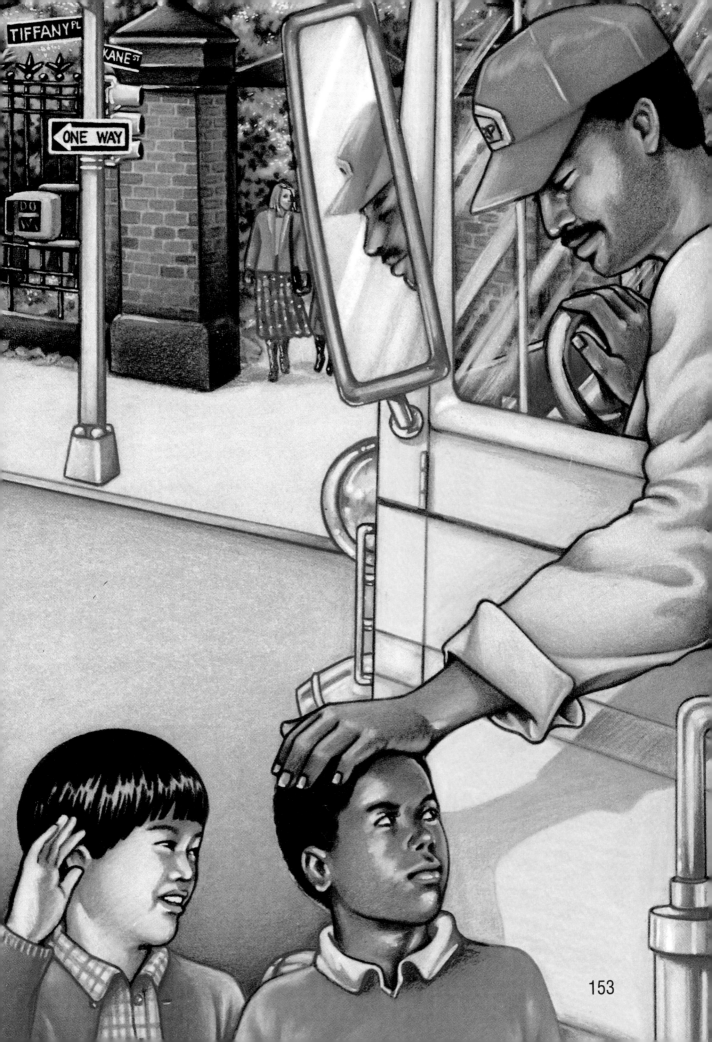

153

154

So Willie stopped hugging his daddy. He never hugged his mama or his sister anymore either. And when they tried to hug Willie, he turned away. But Willie wanted someone to hug. That's what he wanted more than anything.

At school he watched as Miss Mary put her arms around some boy or girl. It didn't look silly. Except when she tried to hug Jo-Jo. Jo-Jo made a big commotion that made everyone laugh. He wriggled and squirmed, and shrieked, "Help! Help! I'm being mugged! Help!"

At night Willie watched his sister pull her teddy bear to her and hug it. She looked so safe and happy lying there with her arms around the bear.

"Why do you hug that old thing?" Willie said. "That's silly."

Rose frowned at Willie. "Who says?" she demanded.

"Jo-Jo says, that's who says," Willie boasted.

"Well, if you ask me, I think Jo-Jo's silly," said Rose. "Besides," she said, squeezing the bear to her, "Homer's nice."

But the next night Willie pinched his nose and said, "What a smelly old bear! I wouldn't hug that old thing for a hundred dollars. Not even for a million dollars. That's silly."

Rose pulled Homer in closer to her. "Willie," she said, "you're just not the hugging kind, then . . . if that's how you feel."

Willie flipped over in bed without even saying, "Good night, sleep tight, God keep you alright." And his mind went around and around on what his sister had said. The words tick-tocked back and forth with the clock sitting on the table by his bed:

NOT-the hugging kind,

NOT-the hugging kind,

NOT-the hugging kind,

if-THAT'S-how-you-feel.

But that was not how Willie felt. More than anything, Willie wanted to be the hugging kind.

Willie watched each morning as his daddy hugged first his mama and then Rose. He remembered how safe and happy he always felt with his daddy's strong arms around him.

He remembered how good it felt to put his arms around his mama. She smelled a little like lemon and a little like the lilac powder in the bathroom. She felt big and a little lumpy. She also felt soft and safe and warm.

One morning Willie went into the kitchen and everyone was hugging everyone else. But no one hugged Willie. They didn't even see him. Willie waited, hoping someone would put their arms around him. If they did, maybe he wouldn't slip away.

But no one tried. Rose just said, when she saw Willie watching, "You know that Willie says he isn't the hugging kind now. He says it's all too, too silly."

"I did not!" said Willie, bristling. "Jo-Jo said that!"

"Oh, but you said it too, Little Brother," Rose said, laughing and tousling his hair.

163

Willie grabbed his lunch and his books, and ran out the door to meet Jo-Jo. "Let's get out of here!" Willie shrieked, breaking into a run. "They're mugging everybody in there!"

That afternoon Jo-Jo's mother picked him up after school, so Willie walked home alone.

He walked through the park and saw a young couple standing on the footbridge with their arms around each other.

He walked down Myrtle Street and saw a woman and a man rushing down the steps from their porch to greet some visitors with hugs all around.

It seemed so long since Willie had had a hug.

He walked into the long, low branches of a willow tree and wrapped his arms around it. A blue jay flew down from a purple plum tree, and Willie reached out to its fluttering wings. He walked up to a stop sign and hugged it.

He hugged his bike in the front yard. He hugged the door to his house when he opened it. And he rushed inside to hug his mama. But she was too busy running the vacuum over the floors. Willie was kind of glad. After all, he felt a little silly.

That night, after Willie had had his bath, he took the old bath towel and draped it across the head of his bed.

"What's that for?" Rose asked, hugging Homer to her.

"Nothing," said Willie.

The next night Willie put the old bath towel on the bed again. And the next night, and the next. Each night, when he was sure that Rose was not watching, he slipped the old towel down from the headboard and he hugged it. But it didn't feel soft and safe and warm.

Willie wanted to hug someONE, not someTHING.

170

In the morning Willie's mama was in the kitchen making biscuits. He watched Rose brush up to her and put her arms around her.

When the biscuits were finished and browning in the oven, Willie went up and put his arms around his mama too. Or almost around her. There was a little more to her than he remembered. She felt much nicer than an old towel. And, even better, she hugged back.

"What's all this, Willie," she said, "hugging around here on me so early in the morning?"

"Yeah, Willie," said Rose. "I thought all that hugging was too, too silly."

Willie clung tighter to his mama.

"That's alright," said his mama. "Willie knows, don't you, Son, that it's them that don't get hugging who think it's silly."

Willie looked up into his mama's face, smiling, until he felt a tap on his shoulder. Turning, he saw his daddy smiling down at him. "My turn, Son," he said.

Willie put his arms around his daddy, burying his face in the familiar khaki shirt and feeling once again secure in the warmth of the strong arms around him.

Breakfast tasted better to Willie than it had in many a day. And when it came time to leave for school, Willie gave hugs all around.

173

Jumping into the big truck, Willie and his daddy stopped by to pick up Jo-Jo. When they arrived at school, Willie reached up and gave his daddy a quick, tight hug. Then he scooted out the door behind Jo-Jo.

"What did you do that for, man?" Jo-Jo said, once they were out of the truck. "Don't you know that's silly?"

Willie gave his friend a shove on the shoulder. Maybe Jo-Jo wouldn't let someone hug him, but he would allow a playful shove now and then. "Go on, now, Jo-Jo," he said. "I think *you're* what's silly."

Jo-Jo ran on ahead. "Help, help!" he shrieked. "I'm being mugged! Help!"

But Willie didn't mind. He lagged behind, feeling warm and safe knowing that he was, after all, the hugging kind.

HUGS and KISSES

Hugs and hugs and kisses . . .
Doesn't she know that I'm a boy?
Hugs and hugs and kisses . . .
I'm not some cuddly toy.

Hugs and hugs and kisses . . .
Boys should be treated rough.
Hugs and hugs and kisses . . .
These muscles show I'm tough.

Hugs and hugs and kisses . . .
Makes me want to run and hide.
I can't show the world how warm . . .
hugs and hugs and kisses
makes me feel
inside.

Lindamichellebaron

A FOLK TALE FROM THE HMONG PEOPLE OF LAOS
TOLD BY BLIA XIONG

NINE▸IN▸ONE, GRR! GRR!

ADAPTED BY CATHY SPAGNOLI
ILLUSTRATED BY NANCY HOM

Many years ago when the earth was nearer the sky than it is today, there lived the first tiger. She and her mate had no babies and so the lonely tiger often thought about the future, wondering how many cubs she would have.

179

Tiger decided to visit the great god Shao, who lived in the sky, who was kind and gentle and knew everything. Surely Shao could tell her how many cubs she would have.

Tiger set out on the road that led to the sky. She climbed through forests of striped bamboo and wild banana trees, past plants curved like rooster tail feathers, and over rocks shaped like sleeping dragons.

At last Tiger came to a stone wall. Beyond the wall was a garden where children played happily under a plum tree. A large house stood nearby, its colorful decorations shining in the sun. This was the land of the great Shao, a peaceful land without sickness or death.

Shao himself came out to greet Tiger. The silver coins dangling from his belt sounded softly as he walked.

"Why did you come here, Tiger?" he asked gently.

"O great Shao," answered Tiger respectfully, "I am lonely and want to know how many cubs I will have."

Shao was silent for a moment. Then he replied, "Nine each year."

"How wonderful," purred Tiger. "Thank you so much, great Shao." And she turned to leave with her good news.

"One moment, Tiger," said Shao. "You must remember carefully what I said. The words alone tell you how many cubs you will have. Do not forget them, for if you do, I cannot help you."

At first Tiger was happy as she followed the road back to earth. But soon, she began to worry.

"Oh dear," she said to herself. "My memory is so bad. How will I ever remember those important words of Shao?" She thought and she thought. At last, she had an idea. "I'll make up a little song to sing. Then I won't forget." So Tiger began to sing:

Nine-in-one, Grr! Grr!
Nine-in-one, Grr! Grr!

Down the mountain went Tiger, past the rocks shaped like sleeping dragons, past the plants curved like rooster tail feathers, through the forests of striped bamboo and wild banana trees. Over and over she sang her song:

Nine-in-one, Grr! Grr!
Nine-in-one, Grr! Grr!

As Tiger came closer to her cave, she passed through clouds of tiny white butterflies. She heard monkeys and barking deer. She saw green-striped snakes, quails and pheasants. None of the animals listened to her song—except one big, clever, black bird, the Eu bird.

"Hmm," said Bird to herself. "I wonder why Tiger is coming down the mountain singing that song and grinning from ear to ear. I'd better find out." So Bird soared up the ladder which was a shortcut to Shao's home.

"wise Shao," asked Bird politely, "why is Tiger singing over and over:

Nine-in-one, Grr! Grr!
Nine-in-one, Grr! Grr!

And Shao explained that he had just told Tiger she would have nine cubs each year.

"That's terrible!" squawked Bird. "If Tiger has nine cubs each year, they will eat all of us. Soon there will be nothing but tigers in the land. You must change what you said, O Shao!"

"I cannot take back my words," sighed Shao. "I promised Tiger that she would have nine cubs every year as long as she remembered my words."

"As long as she remembered your words," repeated Bird thoughtfully. "Then I know what I must do, O great Shao."

Bird now had a plan. She could hardly wait to try it out. Quickly, she returned to earth in search of Tiger.

193

Bird reached her favorite tree as old grandmother sun was setting, just in time to hear Tiger coming closer and closer and still singing:

Nine-in-one, Grr! Grr!
Nine-in-one, Grr! Grr!

Tiger was concentrating so hard on her song that she didn't even see Bird landing in the tree above her.

Suddenly, Bird began to flap her wings furiously. "Flap! Flap! Flap!" went Bird's big, black wings.

"Who's that?" cried Tiger.

"It's only me," answered Bird innocently.

Tiger looked up and growled at Bird:

"Grr! Grr! Bird. You made me forget my song with all your noise."

"h, I can help you," chirped Bird sweetly. "I heard you walking through the woods. You were singing:

**One-in-nine, Grr! Grr!
One-in-nine, Grr! Grr!**

"Oh, thank you, thank you, Bird!" cried Tiger. "I will have one cub every nine years. How wonderful! This time I won't forget!"

197

So Tiger returned to her cave, singing happily:

One-in-nine, Grr! Grr!
One-in-nine, Grr! Grr!

And that is why, the Hmong people say, we don't have too many tigers on the earth today!

MEET BLIA XIONG ◄

Blia Xiong (BLEE-AH SHONG) first heard *Nine-in-One, Grr! Grr!* when she was a little child. She says, "This story was carried in my family for a long time. I was three when I first heard it. I still remember my mother telling me this funny story with a tiger singing in Laotian, 'Nine-in-One, Grr! Grr!'"

In Laos, the tiger is a wild animal that is feared. Some people think the tiger is magical. She says, "The part I like most is when the bird hears the song and figures out how to trick the tiger. The clever bird does something about the powerful tiger."

Blia Xiong was told stories by her mother, her father, and her grandfather before them. Now she tells her children the stories she hears. When asked how she remembers a story, she says, "When I listen to a story, I listen very closely. I make pictures in my mind. Then I can remember what I hear."

MEET NANCY HOM ►

Nancy Hom was born in southern China and grew up in New York City. In addition to *Nine-in-One, Grr! Grr!* she has illustrated the Cambodian folk tale *Judge Rabbit and the Tree Spirit.*

Your Big Backyard
Published by the National Wildlife Federation

May

TIGERS

This tiger's home is in the jungle. It is wet in the jungle, and the plants grow very close together. Tigers hide among the thick plants. There they live and hunt alone.

Tigers eat other animals. They eat antelopes, wild pigs, deer, and fish. Sometimes they even eat crocodiles. Tigers have almost no enemies.

Tigers are very good hunters.

They have soft padded toes so that they can sneak up on animals. Hidden in those toes are the tiger's sharp claws. When the tiger needs its claws to catch dinner, they are ready.

Since tigers are meat eaters, they need strong, sharp teeth. They have teeth for biting and teeth for chewing.

People's teeth are good for biting and chewing too. But they are not as strong as tigers' teeth.

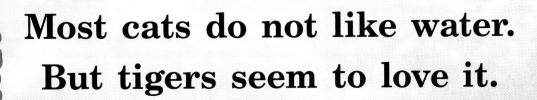

Most cats do not like water.
But tigers seem to love it.

Bees
   own the clover,

birds
   own the sky,

rabbits
   the meadow
   with low grass and high.

Frogs
   own the marshes,

ants
   own the ground . . .
   I hope they don't mind
   my looking around.

                    Aileen Fisher

THE WEDNESDAY SURPRISE

by Eve Bunting

I like surprises. But the one Grandma and I are planning for Dad's birthday is the best surprise of all.

illustrated by Donald Carrick

We work on it Wednesday nights. On Wednesdays Mom has to stay late at the office and my brother, Sam, goes to basketball practice at the Y. That's when Grandma rides the bus across town to stay with me.

I watch for her from the window and I blow on the glass to make breath pictures while I wait. When I see her I call: "Sam! She's here!" and he says it's okay to run down, down the long stairs and wait by the door.

"Grandma!" I call.

"Anna!" She's hurrying, her big, cloth bag bumping against her legs.

We meet and hug. She tells me how much I've grown since last week and I tell her how much she's grown, too, which is our joke. Between us we carry her lumpy bag upstairs.

I show Grandma my breath picture, if it's still there. Mostly she knows what it is. Mostly she's the only one who does.

On Wednesday nights we have hot dogs.

"Have you heard from your dad?" Grandma asks Sam.

"He'll be back Saturday, same as always," Sam says. "In time for his birthday."

"His birthday?" Grandma raises her eyebrows as if she'd forgotten all about that.

Grandma is some actress!

When Sam goes she and I do the dishes. Then we get down to business.

I sit beside her on the couch and she takes the first picture book from the bag. We read the story together, out loud, and when we finish one book we start a second.

We read for an hour, get some ice cream, then read some more.

Grandma gives me another hug. "Only seven years old and smart as paint already!"

I'm pleased. "They're all going to be so surprised on Saturday," I say.

When Sam comes home we play card games, and when Mom comes she plays, too.

"You'll be here for the birthday dinner?" Mom asks as Grandma is getting ready to leave.

"Oh yes, the birthday," Grandma says vaguely, as if she'd forgotten again. As if we hadn't been working on our special surprise for weeks and weeks. Grandma is tricky.

"I'll be here," she says.

Sam walks Grandma to the bus stop. As they're going down the stairs I hear him say: "What have you got in this bag, Grandma? Bricks?"

That makes me smile.

Dad comes home Saturday morning, and we rush at him with our *Happy Birthdays*. He has brought Sam a basketball magazine and me a pebble, smooth and speckled as an egg, for my rock collection.

"I found it in the desert, close to the truck stop," he says. "It was half covered with sand."

I hold it, imagining I can still feel the desert sun hot inside it. How long did it lie there? What kind of rock is it?

ad has stopped to pick wildflowers for Mom. They're wilting and she runs to put them in water. Then Dad has to go to bed because he has been driving his big truck all through the night.

While Dad sleeps, Sam and I hang red and blue streamers in the living room. We help Mom frost the cake. We've made Dad's favorite dinner, pot roast, and our gifts are wrapped and ready.

I watch for Grandma and help carry the bag upstairs. Wow! Sam should feel how heavy it is now! Grandma has brought a ton of books. We hide the bag behind the couch. I am sick from being nervous.

Grandma usually has seconds but tonight she doesn't. I don't either. I can tell Mom is worried about the pot roast but Grandma tells her it's very good.

"Are you feeling well, Mama?" Dad asks Grandma. "How are your knees?"

"Fine. Fine. The knees are fine."

Dad blows out the birthday candles and we give him his gifts. Then Grandma shoots a glance in my direction and I go for the big bag and drag it across to the table. I settle it on the floor between us.

"Another present?" Dad asks.

"It's a special surprise for your birthday, Dad, from Grandma and me."

My heart's beating awfully fast as I unzip the bag and give the first book to Grandma. It's called *Popcorn*. I squeeze Grandma's hand and she stands and begins to read.

Mom and Dad and Sam are all astonished.

Dad jumps up and says: "What's this?" but Mom shushes him and pulls him back down.

Grandma has the floor. She finishes *Popcorn*, which takes quite a while, gives the book back to me and beams all over her face.

"My goodness!" Mom is beaming too. "When did this wonderful thing happen? When did you learn to read?"

"Anna taught me," Grandma says.

"On Wednesday nights," I add. "And she took the books home, and practiced."

"You were always telling me to go to classes, classes, classes," Grandma says to Dad. She looks at Mom. "You must learn to read, you say. So? I come to Anna."

I giggle because I'm so excited.

Grandma reads and acts out *The Easter Pig.* And *The Velveteen Rabbit.*

"It's much smarter if you learn to read when you're young," she tells Sam sternly. "The chance may pass along with the years."

Sam looks hurt. "But I *can* read, Grandma."

"Nevertheless." She takes out another book.

"Are you going to read everything in that bag, Mama?" Dad asks her. He's grinning, but his eyes are brimming over with tears and he and Mom are holding hands across the table.

"Maybe I will read everything in the world now that I've started," Grandma says in a stuck-up way. "I've got time." She winks at me.

"So, Anna? What do you think? Was it a good surprise?"

I run to her and she puts her cheek against mine. "The best ever," I say.

Meet
Eve Bunting

There's a story about *The Wednesday Surprise,* and Eve Bunting tells about it like this: "A friend took me out to dinner and began talking about her mother, Katina, who was quite a character.

"She told a story about how she taught her mother to read English with her picture books. Every day she would bring books home from school or the library, and they would read them together. *The Wednesday Surprise* is my book, but it's Katina's story."

Ms. Bunting loves Donald Carrick's illustrations. She asked him if the kitchen in *The Wednesday Surprise* was like his kitchen. He said to her, "Oh, yes. There's always a bit of my house in my books."

Meet DONALD CARRICK

Donald Carrick started drawing pictures as a child, and he kept on drawing his whole life. His first job was painting signs and billboards. Later, he painted pictures for newspaper and magazine ads. His wife, Carol, wrote the first children's book he ever illustrated, *The Old Barn.* After that, Donald Carrick illustrated more than eighty picture books. Some of the most popular ones are about a boy named Christopher and his two dogs. Two other well-known books are about a boy named Patrick who imagines there are dinosaurs everywhere.

WHAT in the WORLD?

EVE MERRIAM

What in the world
  goes whiskery friskery
    meowling and prowling
      napping and lapping
        at silky milk?
Psst
What is it?

What in the world
  goes leaping and beeping
    onto a lily pad onto a log
      onto a tree stump or down to the bog?
Splash, blurp,
Kerchurp!

What in the world
  goes gnawing and pawing
    scratching and latching
      sniffing and squiffing
        nibbling for tidbits of left-over cheese?
Please?

What in the world
   jumps with a hop and a bump
      and a tail that can thump
         has pink pointy ears and a twitchy nose
            looking for anything crunchy that grows?
A carroty lettucey cabbagey luncheon
To munch on?

What in the world
   climbs chattering pattering swinging from trees
      like a flying trapeze
         with a tail that can curl
            like the rope the cowboys twirl?
Wahoo!
Here's a banana for you!

What in the world
   goes stalking and balking
      running and sunning
         thumping and dumping
            lugging and hugging
               swinging and singing
                  wriggling and giggling
                     sliding and hiding
                        throwing and knowing and
                           growing and growing
                              much too big for
                                 last year's clothes?

Who knows?

Unit 3

The MYSTERIOUS Tadpole

by Steven Kellogg

ncle McAllister lived in Scotland.

Every year he sent Louis a birthday
gift for his nature collection.

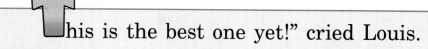

"This is the best one yet!" cried Louis.

The next day he took his entire collection to school for show-and-tell.

"Class, this is a tadpole," said Mrs. Shelbert. She asked Louis to bring it back often so they could all watch it become a frog.

HOW THE TADPOLE BECOMES THE FROG

1. ____
2. ____
3. ____
4. ____
5.

1. ⊙
2. ∼
3.
4.
5.
6.

A RED HEADED WISE OWL
by Fredrick

A VERY ANGRY GROUSE
PECK PECK PECK PECK PECK

geese who are lost

A CARDINAL is HAPPY
by MARIE

HERE IS the EAGLE
BY LUCY

Louis named the tadpole Alphonse. Every day Alphonse ate several cheeseburgers.

Louis found that he was eager to learn.

When Alphonse became too big for his jar, Louis moved him to the sink.

After Alphonse outgrew the sink, Louis's parents agreed to let him use the bathtub.

One day Mrs. Shelbert decided that Alphonse was not turning into an ordinary frog.

She asked Louis to stop bringing him to school.

By the time summer vacation arrived,
Alphonse was enormous.

"He's too big for the bathtub,"
said Louis's mother.

"He's too big for the apartment,"
said Louis's father.

"He needs a swimming pool," said Louis.

"There is no place in our apartment for a
swimming pool," said his parents.

244

ouis suggested that they buy the parking lot next door and build a swimming pool.

"It would cost more money than we have," said his parents. "Your tadpole will have to be donated to the zoo."

The thought of Alphonse in a cage made Louis very sad.

hen, in the middle of the night, Louis remembered that the junior high had a swimming pool that nobody used during the summer.

Louis hid Alphonse under a rug and smuggled him into the school.

After making sure that Alphonse felt at home, Louis went back to bed.

Every morning Louis spent several hours swimming with his friend. In the afternoon he earned the money for Alphonse's cheeseburgers by delivering newspapers.

Meanwhile the training continued. Alphonse learned to retrieve things from the bottom of the pool.

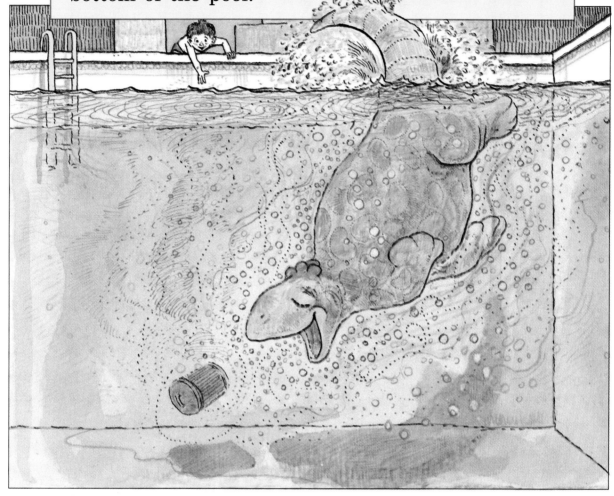

Summer vacation passed quickly. Louis worried what would happen to Alphonse now that school had reopened.

As soon as the first day ended, he ran to the junior high. The students were getting ready for after-school activities.

ouis arrived just as the first swimming race began.

Alphonse was delighted to see all the swimmers.

"It's a submarine from another planet!" bellowed the coach. "Call the police! Call the Navy!"

"No! It's a tadpole!" cried Louis. "He's my pet!"

The coach was upset and confused.

"You have until tomorrow," he cried, "to get that creature out of the pool!"

Louis didn't know what to do. On the way home he met his friend Miss Seevers, the librarian, and he told her his problem.

Miss Seevers went back to the junior high school with Louis, but when she saw Alphonse, she was so shocked that she dropped her purse and the books she was carrying into the swimming pool. Alphonse retrieved them.

hen Miss Seevers telephoned Louis's Uncle McAllister in Scotland. He told her that he had caught the little tadpole in Loch Ness, a large lake near his cottage.

Miss Seevers said, "I'm convinced that your uncle has given you a very rare Loch Ness monster!"

"I don't care!" cried Louis. "He's my pet, and I love him!" He begged Miss Seevers to help him raise enough money to buy the parking lot near his apartment so he could build a swimming pool for Alphonse.

Suddenly Miss Seevers had an idea.

"In 1639 there was a battle in our city's harbor," she said. "A pirate treasure ship was sunk, and no one has ever been able to find it. But perhaps we can!"

The next morning Miss Seevers and Louis rented a boat.

In the middle of the harbor Louis showed Alphonse a picture of a treasure chest.

Alphonse disappeared under the water.

Louis and Miss Seevers bought the parking lot.

They hired some helpers.

259

And when the pool was completed, all

260

the children in the city were invited to swim.

That night Louis said, "Alphonse, next week is my birthday, which means that we've been friends for almost a year."

Far away in Scotland Uncle McAllister was also thinking about the approaching birthday. While out hiking he discovered an unusual stone in a clump of grass and sticks.

"A perfect gift for my nephew!" he cried.

"I'll deliver it in person!"

ncle McAllister arrived at Louis's apartment and gave Louis the present.

Louis couldn't wait to add it to his collection.

Suddenly a crack appeared in the stone. . . .

Meet Steven Kellogg

When asked why he wrote *The Mysterious Tadpole,* Steven Kellogg said, "My parents weren't enthusiastic about having animals in the home. But I loved animals as a child, and I still do."

He added, "I have always been fascinated with the Loch Ness monster. I like it because it remains mysterious. I always wonder if there are young ones. Are they tadpoles?"

But Mr. Kellogg says this is not just a book about having a pet or the Loch Ness monster. He says, "This book is about friendship. Alphonse is unacceptable to the parents and the teacher, but not to Louis. Louis loves him so much that he tries to make his friend a part of his life."

PUPPY AND I

I met a man as I went walking;
We got talking,
Man and I.
"Where are you going to, Man?" I said
(I said to the Man as he went by).
"Down to the village, to get some bread.
Will you come with me?" "No, not I."

I met a Horse as I went walking;
We got talking,
Horse and I.
"Where are you going to, Horse, to-day?"
(I said to the Horse as he went by).
"Down to the village to get some hay.
Will you come with me?" "No, not I."

I met a Woman as I went walking;
We got talking,
Woman and I.
"Where are you going to, Woman, so early?"
(I said to the Woman as she went by).
"Down to the village to get some barley.
Will you come with me?" "No, not I."

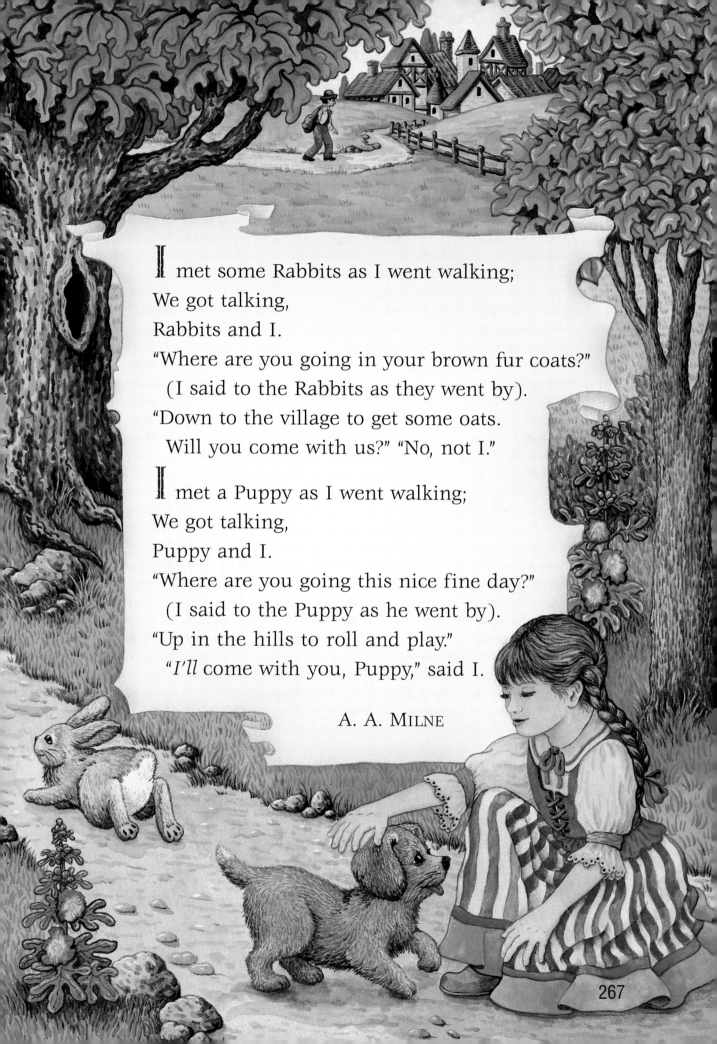

I met some Rabbits as I went walking;
We got talking,
Rabbits and I.
"Where are you going in your brown fur coats?"
  (I said to the Rabbits as they went by).
"Down to the village to get some oats.
  Will you come with us?" "No, not I."

I met a Puppy as I went walking;
We got talking,
Puppy and I.
"Where are you going this nice fine day?"
  (I said to the Puppy as he went by).
"Up in the hills to roll and play."
  "*I'll* come with you, Puppy," said I.

A. A. MILNE

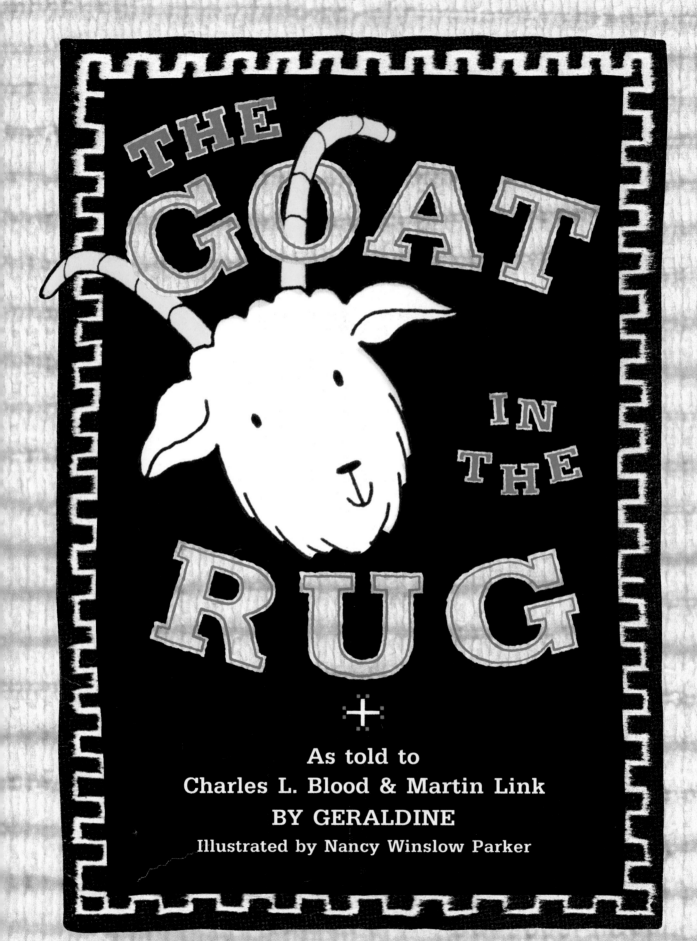

THE GOAT IN THE RUG

✦

As told to
Charles L. Blood & Martin Link
BY GERALDINE
Illustrated by Nancy Winslow Parker

My name is Geraldine and I live near a place called Window Rock with my Navajo friend, Glenmae. It's called Window Rock because it has a big round hole in it that looks like a window open to the sky.

Glenmae is called Glenmae most of the time because it's easier to say than her Indian name: Glee 'Nasbah. In English that means something like female warrior, but she's really a Navajo weaver. I guess that's why, one day, she decided to weave me into a rug.

I remember it was a warm, sunny afternoon. Glenmae had spent most of the morning sharpening a large pair of scissors. I had no idea what she was going to use them for, but it didn't take me long to find out.

Before I knew what was happening,
I was on the ground and Glenmae was
clipping off my wool in great long strands.
(It's called mohair, really.) It didn't hurt at all,
but I admit I kicked up my heels some. I'm
very ticklish for a goat.

I might have looked a little naked and silly afterwards, but my, did I feel nice and cool! So I decided to stick around and see what would happen next.

The first thing Glenmae did was chop up roots from a yucca plant. The roots made a soapy, rich lather when she mixed them with water.

She washed my wool in the suds until it was clean and white.

After that, a little bit of me (you might say) was hung up in the sun to dry. When my wool was dry, Glenmae took out two large square combs with many teeth.

By combing my wool between these carding combs, as they're called, she removed any bits of twigs or burrs and straightened out the fibers. She told me it helped make a smoother yarn for spinning.

Then, Glenmae carefully started to spin my wool—one small bundle at a time—into yarn. I was beginning to find out it takes a long while to make a Navajo rug.

Again and again, Glenmae twisted and pulled, twisted and pulled the wool. Then she spun it around a long, thin stick she called a spindle. As she twisted and pulled and spun, the finer, stronger and smoother the yarn became.

A few days later, Glenmae and I went for a walk. She said we were going to find some special plants she would use to make dye.

I didn't know what "dye" meant, but it sounded like a picnic to me. I do love to eat plants. That's what got me into trouble.

rabbitbrush
wild onion
cliffrose
sumac
juniper
walnuts
dock

277

While Glenmae was out looking for more plants, I ate every one she had already collected in her bucket. Delicious!

The next day, Glenmae made me stay home while she walked miles to a store. She said the dye she could buy wasn't the same as the kind she makes from plants, but since I'd made such a pig of myself, it would have to do.

I was really worried that she would still be angry with me when she got back. She wasn't, though, and pretty soon she had three big potfuls of dye boiling over a fire.

Then I saw what Glenmae had meant by dyeing. She dipped my white wool into one pot . . . and it turned pink! She dipped it in again. It turned a darker pink! By the time she'd finished dipping it in and out and hung it up to dry, it was a beautiful deep red.

After that, she dyed some of my wool brown, and some of it black. I couldn't help wondering if those plants I'd eaten would turn all of me the same colors.

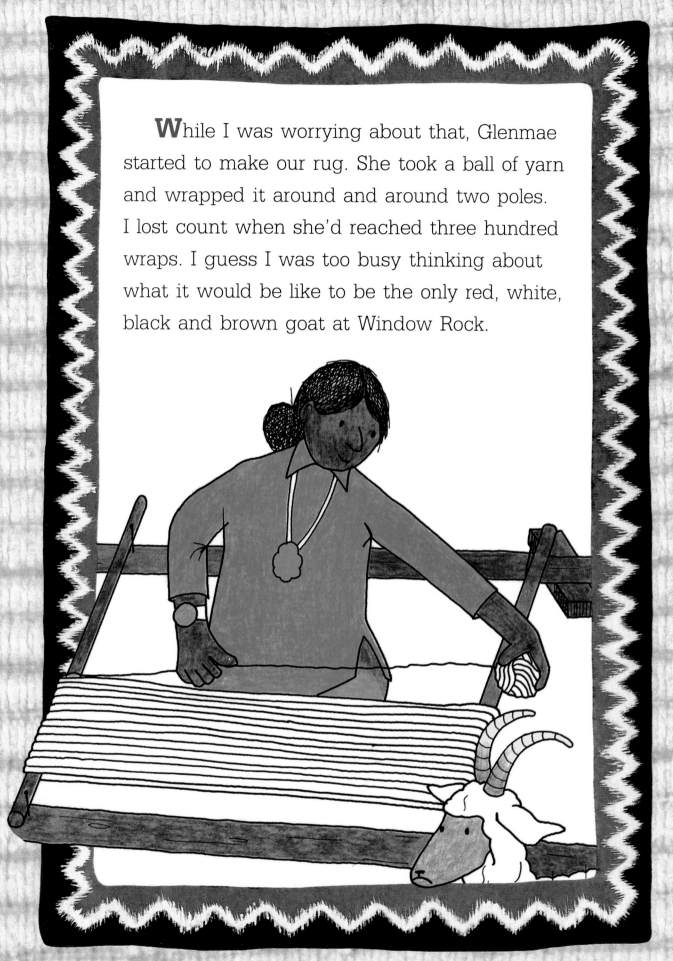

While I was worrying about that, Glenmae started to make our rug. She took a ball of yarn and wrapped it around and around two poles. I lost count when she'd reached three hundred wraps. I guess I was too busy thinking about what it would be like to be the only red, white, black and brown goat at Window Rock.

It wasn't long before Glenmae had finished wrapping. Then she hung the poles with the yarn on a big wooden frame. It looked like a picture frame made of logs—she called it a "loom."

After a whole week of getting ready to weave, Glenmae started. She began weaving at the bottom of the loom. Then, one strand of yarn at a time, our rug started growing toward the top.

A few strands of black.

A few of brown.

A few of red.

In and out. Back and forth.

Until, in a few days, the pattern of our rug was clear to see.

Our rug grew very slowly. Just as every Navajo weaver before her had done for hundreds and hundreds of years, Glenmae formed a design that would never be duplicated.

Then, at last, the weaving was finished! But not until I'd checked it quite thoroughly in front . . .

. . . and in back, did I let Glenmae take our rug off the loom.

There was a lot of me in that rug. I wanted it to be perfect. And it was.

Since then, my wool has grown almost long enough for Glenmae and me to make another rug. I hope we do very soon. Because, you see, there aren't too many weavers like Glenmae left among the Navajos.

And there's only one goat like me, Geraldine.

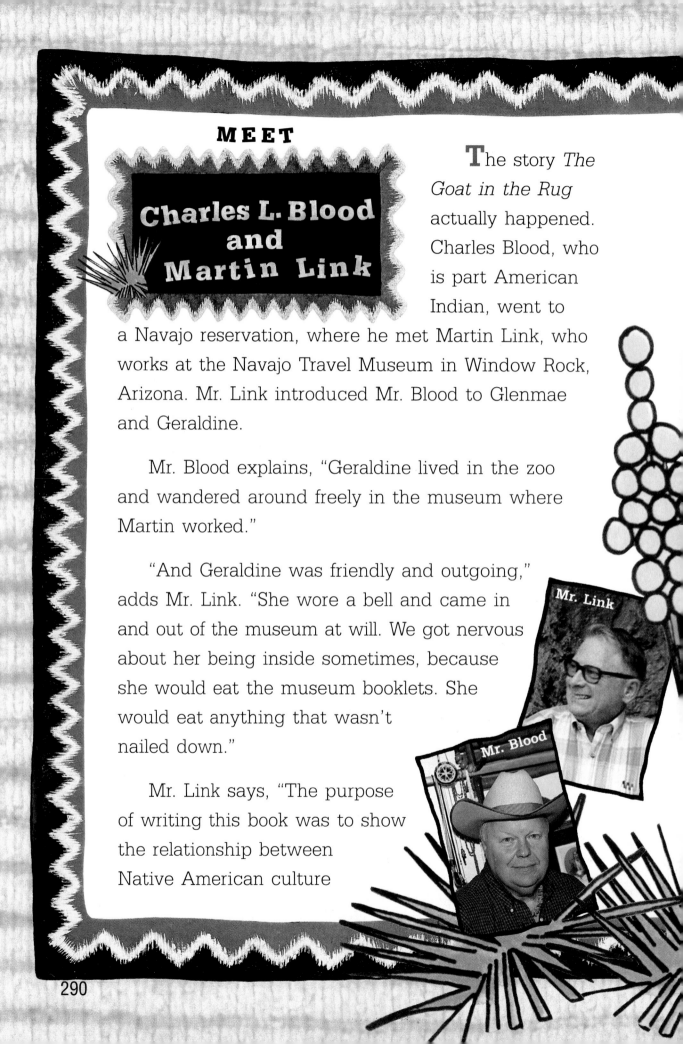

MEET
Charles L. Blood and Martin Link

The story *The Goat in the Rug* actually happened. Charles Blood, who is part American Indian, went to a Navajo reservation, where he met Martin Link, who works at the Navajo Travel Museum in Window Rock, Arizona. Mr. Link introduced Mr. Blood to Glenmae and Geraldine.

Mr. Blood explains, "Geraldine lived in the zoo and wandered around freely in the museum where Martin worked."

"And Geraldine was friendly and outgoing," adds Mr. Link. "She wore a bell and came in and out of the museum at will. We got nervous about her being inside sometimes, because she would eat the museum booklets. She would eat anything that wasn't nailed down."

Mr. Link says, "The purpose of writing this book was to show the relationship between Native American culture

Mr. Link

Mr. Blood

and the animal world. Native Americans know how to live in harmony and cooperation with the animals. They can teach us how to do this."

"When I first saw *The Goat in the Rug,* I knew I wanted to draw pictures for it," said Nancy Winslow Parker. "I spent a lot of time looking at exhibits in museums to find out about the Navajos. I also read a lot of books about weaving and studied Navajo rugs and clothes. I used what I learned to make the border designs and the clothes Glenmae wears."

MEET

Nancy Winslow Parker

The authors also helped Ms. Parker. "Mr. Link and Mr. Blood gave me photographs of a weaver on a Navajo reservation in Window Rock," she explains. "The photographs helped me a lot."

A Wool Surprise for Kenji

by Sue Katharine Jackson   art by Dora Leder

colored thread

fabric scraps

vat for dying wool

dyed wool

spinning wheel

raw wool

loom

skeins of spun wool

Kenji's grandmother, Mabs, is a weaver. Kenji likes to spend time with Mabs in her studio. On cold days, Mabs lights the wood stove to warm the studio while she and Kenji work together.

Sometimes Kenji just looks through bags of wool. Some bags have fluffy bunches of natural grays, blacks, browns, and whites. Other bags have wool that has been cleaned, carded, and dyed different colors. Kenji holds the soft clumps to his cheek while Mabs tells him about the animals the wool comes from.

Romney sheep

llama

alpaca

collie

knitting machine

carder

Kenji wishes he could try making the big looms *click clack* the way Mabs does. Mabs says, "Please don't play with the loom, Kenji." But she doesn't mind if he pushes the foot pedal that makes the spinning wheel spin. And when she cards wool to comb and clean it, Kenji turns the crank to operate the carder. He likes to help her.

293

One afternoon Mabs and Kenji work on a special
project together. Mabs pulls a bunch of white wool
out of one bag and asks Kenji to choose some
colored pieces from another. Mabs fills a
bucket with soapy, warm water
and pulls two stools up to
the bucket.

Mabs cups the wool tightly in her
hands and dips it into the warm, soapy water.
She squeezes the wool into a round shape and begins patting,
rubbing, pressing, and shaping the wool pieces. She gives Kenji
the wet, heavy ball and shows him how to pat it, turn it, press
it, rub it, and squeeze it. The wet, soft but scratchy wool
tickles Kenji's hands, and he laughs.

Kenji and Mabs take turns dipping the wool into the bucket and then patting, rubbing, and rounding it. Soon the separate wool pieces begin to hold together in a firm shape. Kenji and Mabs keep working.

Finally Mabs tells Kenji that they are done. "We made a felt ball," she says as she hands Kenji the still-warm, heavy, wet ball. "Let's put it in the dryer for a while." They eat lunch while the felt ball dries. When they take the ball out of the dryer, it feels light and strong. The wool pieces cannot be separated. Kenji practices throwing the ball all over Mabs's yard. He is very proud of the felt ball he and Mabs made.

My Horse, Fly Like a Bird

My horse, fly like a bird

To carry me far

From the arrows of my enemies,

And I will tie red ribbons

To your streaming hair.

Virginia Driving Hawk Sneve
adapted from
a Lakota warrior's
song to his horse

This photograph shows part of a beaded bag made by a Cheyenne River Sioux, somewhere between the years 1885 and 1890. The beads are sewn on a hide and show the Miniconjou chief White Swan.

297

HEY, BUG!

Hey, bug, stay!
Don't run away.
I know a game that we can play.

I'll hold my fingers very still
and you can climb a finger-hill.

No, no.
Don't go.

Here's a wall—a tower, too,
a tiny bug town, just for you.
I've a cookie. You have some.
Take this oatmeal cookie crumb.

Hey, bug, stay!
Hey, bug!
Hey!

Lilian Moore

HENRY'S

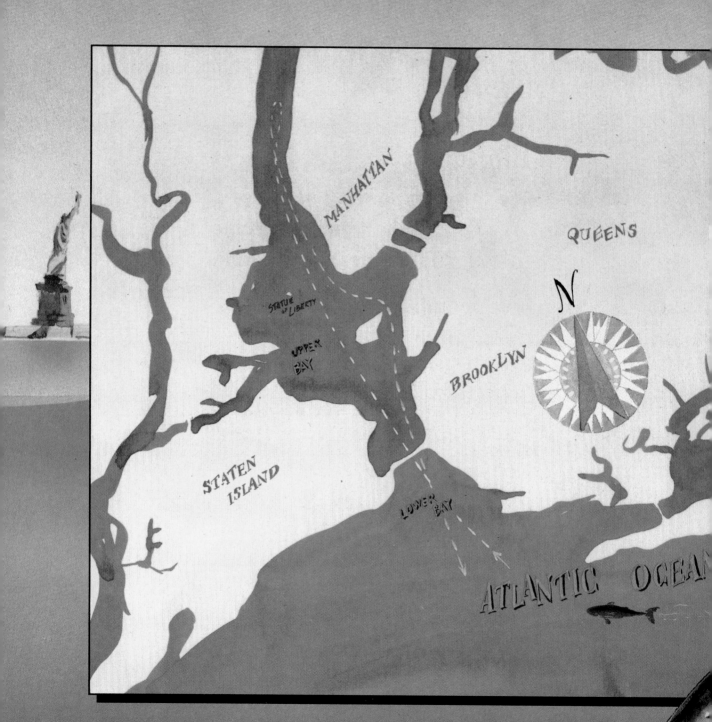

WRONG TURN

WRITTEN BY
HARRIET ZIEFERT

ILLUSTRATED BY
ANDREA BARUFFI

LONG ISLAND

He was a big humpback whale who made a wrong turn. He was swimming in the ocean, and instead of going out to sea, he turned and went up the Hudson River—right into New York Harbor.

No one knew why Henry—for that is what someone named him—wanted to be in New York Harbor. Certainly there was nothing for him to eat in those waters. But there he was.

Henry swam under the Verrazano-Narrows
Bridge. The day was bright and sunny, and on
the bridge, traffic moved right along. No one
up there noticed Henry, but down in the harbor,
a tugboat captain did. He signaled to all the
other boats: *Watch out for the whale!*

There was lots of excitement. No one could remember seeing a whale in New York Harbor. Everyone was on the lookout for Henry. But where was he?

"Look! There he is!" shouted one of the visitors to the Statue of Liberty. "Take a good look, everyone, because you probably won't see another one like him again."

The *Queen Elizabeth 2* passed
Henry on her way to sea. He was
quite small next to the mighty liner.
The ship sounded its horn and
Henry again dove under the water.

The Coast Guard wanted to help
Henry, so they sent a boat to
follow him.

Henry quickly swam away from the patrol boat. He passed an aircraft carrier, *Intrepid*. Visitors on deck cheered when Henry sent up a magnificent spray.

Suddenly, Henry disappeared.

311

No one saw Henry until evening. By then he was near the World Trade Center. He seemed lost. "We've got to help Henry go back to the ocean," the Coast Guard sailors told each other. "There are too many boats in the harbor. He could get hit!"

In the twilight, Henry headed past the
Battery into Buttermilk Channel between
Governors Island and Red Hook in Brooklyn.

Two ferries carrying commuters were just leaving their slips. The ferries immediately put their engines in reverse, veered off their courses and . . . avoided a collision with Henry!

COAST GUARD

Now the Coast Guard was back on Henry's tail. The captain of the cutter was determined to make him turn around and return to the ocean.

And it worked! Perhaps Henry didn't like the noise from the boat's engines. Perhaps he was hungry. For whatever reason, Henry turned around.

Henry swam fast. By the time the moon was
in the sky, he was back at the Verrazano-Narrows
Bridge, heading out to sea.

Henry left the
harbor, then he dove.
"Good luck, Henry!"

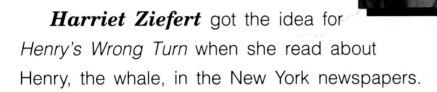

Harriet Ziefert got the idea for *Henry's Wrong Turn* when she read about Henry, the whale, in the New York newspapers.

Harriet Ziefert decided not to make up what Henry was thinking and feeling. "We don't know why whales sometimes do what Henry did," she says. "We just know that sometimes they get confused."

Ms. Ziefert has written more than a hundred books for children. She tells children, "The more you write, the easier it becomes to write stories."

AND ANDREA BARUFFI

Andrea Baruffi came to the United States from Italy. He says, "*Henry's Wrong Turn* was an exciting book for me because I was painting something that really happened. I live on the Hudson River where the story happened."

For this book, it was important for Mr. Baruffi to show New York Harbor. "One day I took a trip on a boat to see how I should paint the ferries," he says.

321

WHALE WATCH

Where Do They Go?

A humpback whale that swims in the Pacific Ocean spends its summer off the coast of Alaska. It travels to the waters of Hawaii, a journey of about 3,000 miles (5,556 kilometers), or Mexico, a journey of about 3,381 miles (6,262 kilometers), for the winter.

A humpback whale that swims in the Atlantic Ocean feeds during the summer near Maine, Canada, Greenland, or Iceland. In the winter, it travels to Puerto Rico or the tip of South America, a journey of about 11,433 miles (18,396 kilometers).

Greenland

Iceland

Alaska

Canada

Maine

ATLANTIC OCEAN

North America

Mexico

Puerto Rico

Hawaii

PACIFIC OCEAN

South America

Today, there are about 10,000 humpback whales. A hundred years ago, before hunters killed many of them, there were ten times that number. Now, laws protect humpback whales from hunters.

I have a little turtle
Name of Myrtle.
I have an extra lizard
Name of Wizard.
I have two kinds of snake:
Bill and Blake.
I have a dandy hutch
Without the rabbit.
If you see any such,
Will you please grab it?

David McCord

325

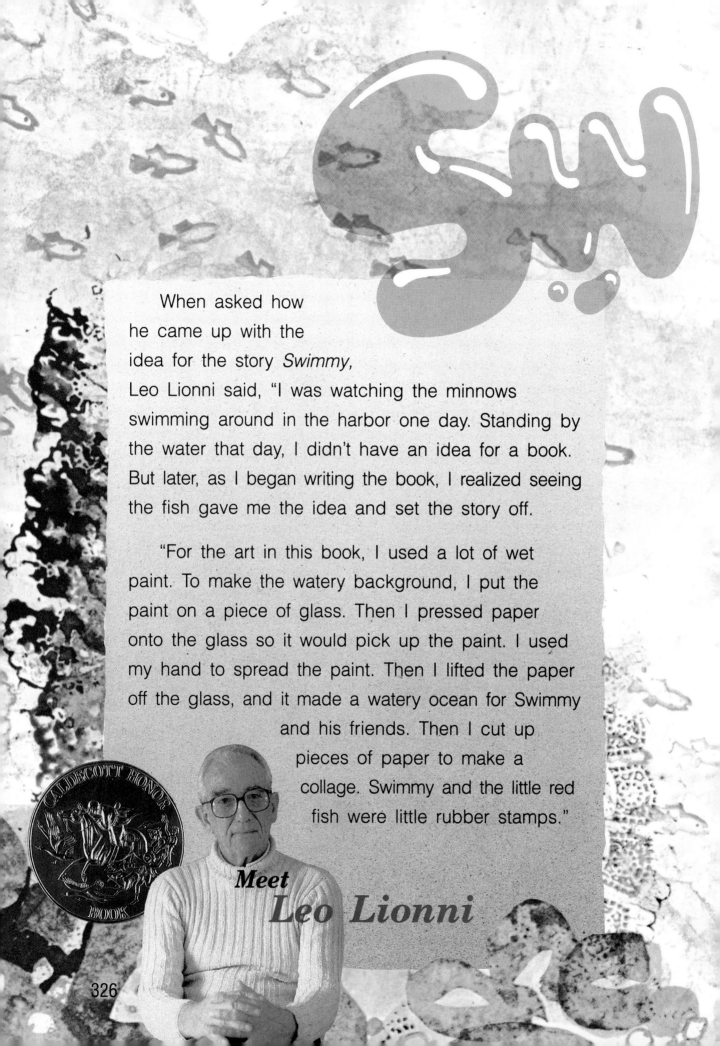

When asked how he came up with the idea for the story *Swimmy,* Leo Lionni said, "I was watching the minnows swimming around in the harbor one day. Standing by the water that day, I didn't have an idea for a book. But later, as I began writing the book, I realized seeing the fish gave me the idea and set the story off.

"For the art in this book, I used a lot of wet paint. To make the watery background, I put the paint on a piece of glass. Then I pressed paper onto the glass so it would pick up the paint. I used my hand to spread the paint. Then I lifted the paper off the glass, and it made a watery ocean for Swimmy and his friends. Then I cut up pieces of paper to make a collage. Swimmy and the little red fish were little rubber stamps."

Meet
Leo Lionni

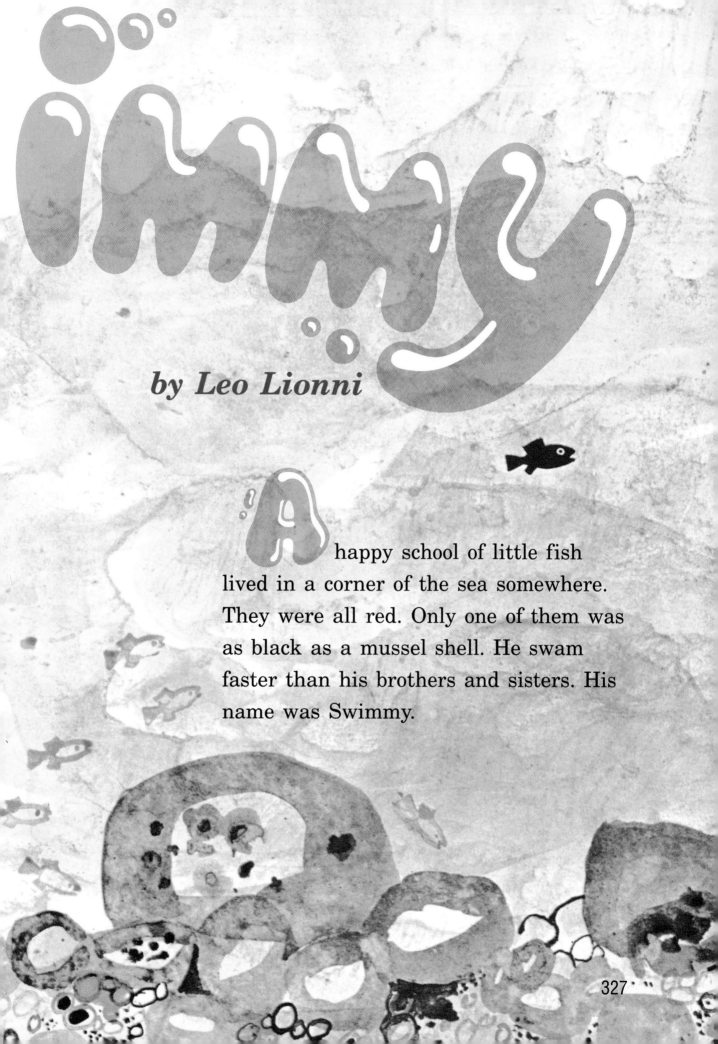

Swimmy

by Leo Lionni

A happy school of little fish lived in a corner of the sea somewhere. They were all red. Only one of them was as black as a mussel shell. He swam faster than his brothers and sisters. His name was Swimmy.

One bad day a tuna fish, swift, fierce and very hungry, came darting through the waves. In one gulp he swallowed all the little red fish.

Only Swimmy escaped. He swam away in the deep wet world. He was scared, lonely and very sad.

But the sea was full of wonderful creatures, and as he swam from marvel to marvel Swimmy was happy again.

He saw a medusa made of rainbow jelly...

a lobster, who walked about like a
water-moving machine . . .

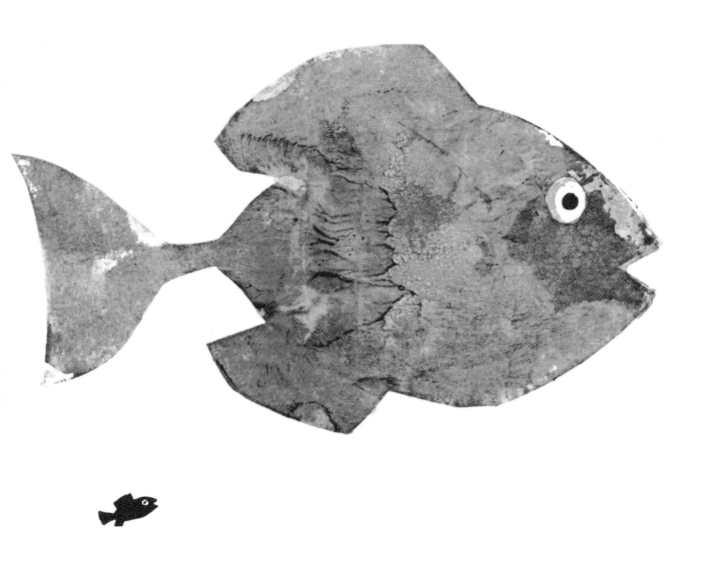

strange fish, pulled by an invisible thread . . .

335

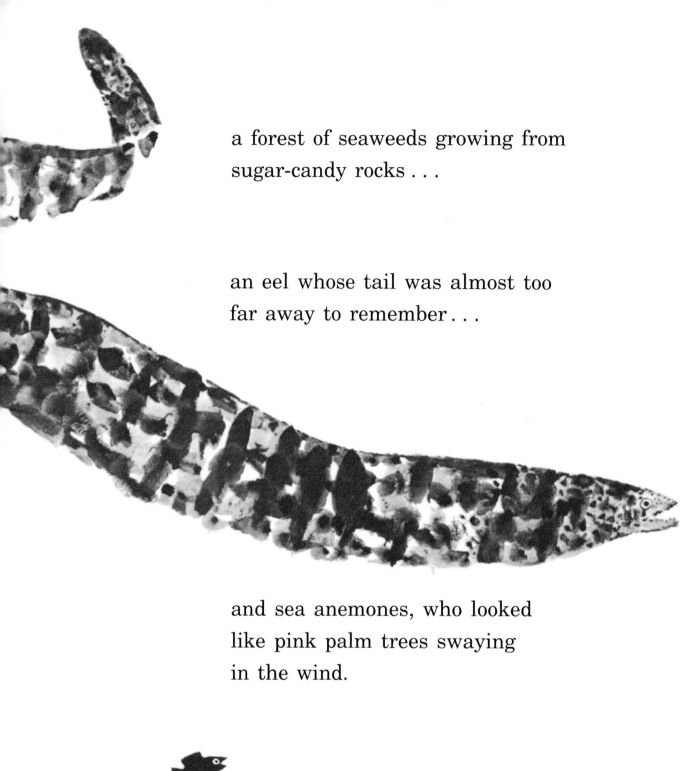

a forest of seaweeds growing from
sugar-candy rocks . . .

an eel whose tail was almost too
far away to remember . . .

and sea anemones, who looked
like pink palm trees swaying
in the wind.

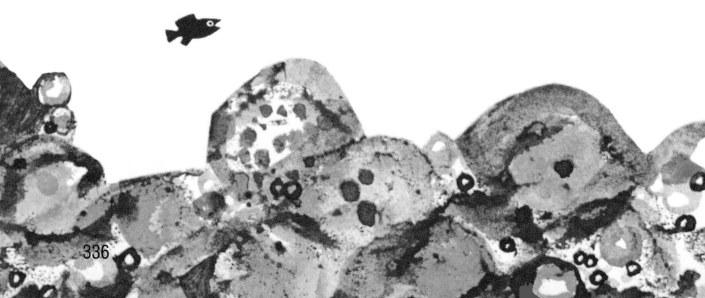

Then, hidden in the dark shade of rocks and weeds, he saw a school of little fish, just like his own.

"Let's go and swim and play and SEE things!" he said happily.

"We can't," said the little red fish. "The big fish will eat us all."

"But you can't just lie there," said Swimmy. "We must THINK of something."

Swimmy thought and thought and thought. Then suddenly he said, "I have it! We are going to swim all together like the biggest fish in the sea!"

He taught them to swim close together, each in his own place, and when they had learned to swim like one giant fish, he said, "I'll be the eye."

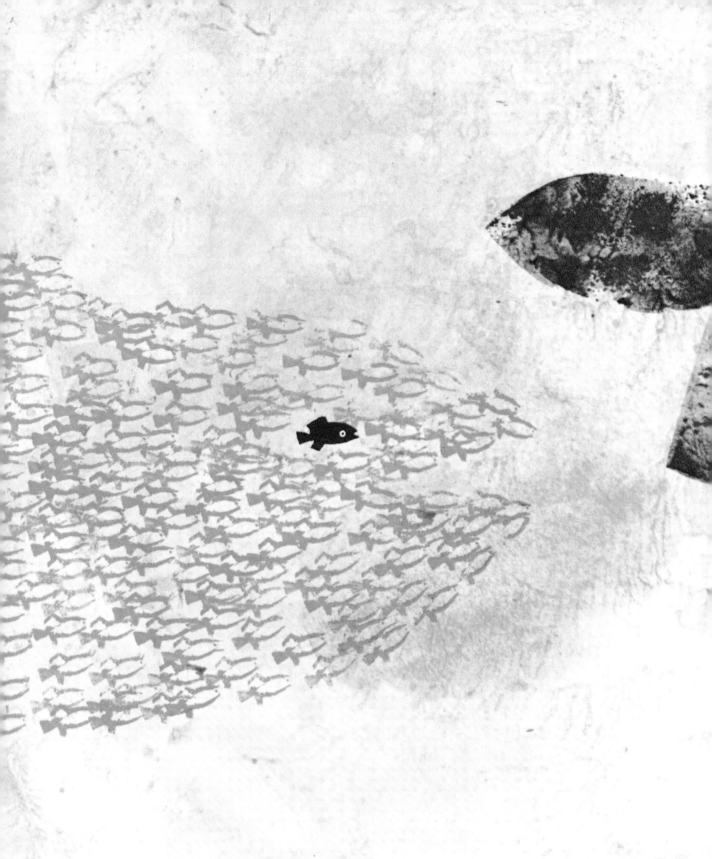

And so they swam in the cool morning water and
in the midday sun and chased the big fish away.

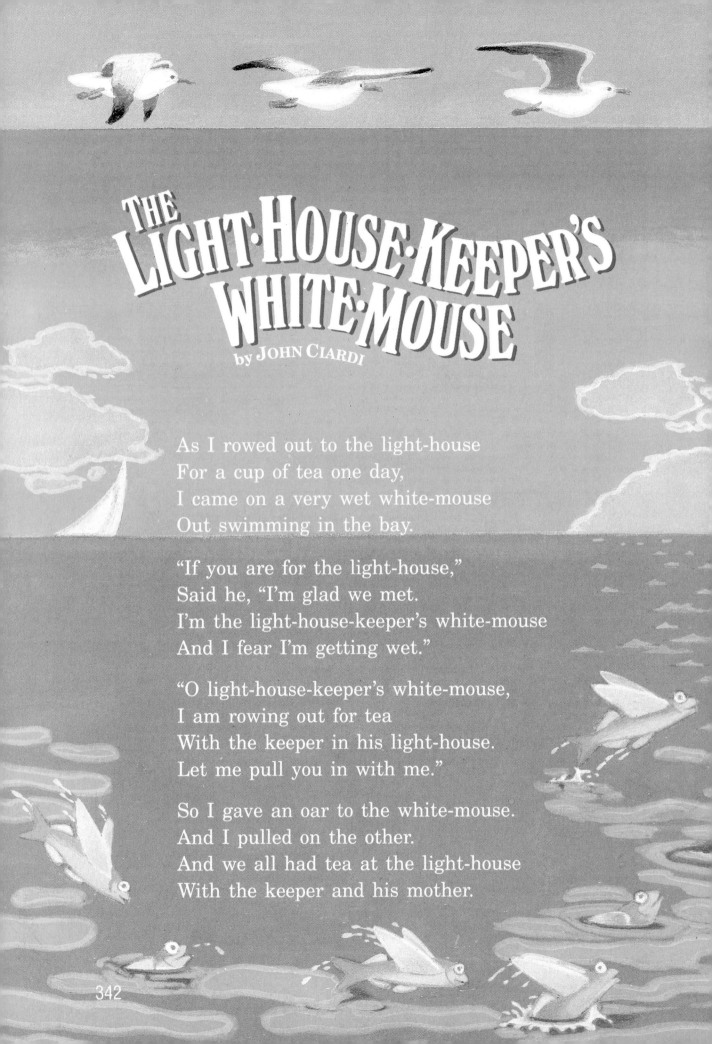

THE LIGHT·HOUSE·KEEPER'S WHITE·MOUSE

by JOHN CIARDI

As I rowed out to the light-house
For a cup of tea one day,
I came on a very wet white-mouse
Out swimming in the bay.

"If you are for the light-house,"
Said he, "I'm glad we met.
I'm the light-house-keeper's white-mouse
And I fear I'm getting wet."

"O light-house-keeper's white-mouse,
I am rowing out for tea
With the keeper in his light-house.
Let me pull you in with me."

So I gave an oar to the white-mouse.
And I pulled on the other.
And we all had tea at the light-house
With the keeper and his mother.

Reading Resources

CONTENTS

Book Parts

TITLE PAGE

HENRY AND MUDGE
AND THE
Bedtime Thumps

The Ninth Book of Their Adventures

Story by Cynthia Rylant
Pictures by Suçie Stevenson

BRADBURY PRESS • NEW YORK

Collier Macmillan Canada • Toronto
Maxwell Macmillan International Publishing Group
New York • Oxford • Singapore • Sydney

Contents

**TABLE OF
CONTENTS**

Book Parts

INDEX

Brochures

WELCOME TO THE Aquarium

Dive right in! Discover marine life from the depths of the ocean to the surface of a backyard pond. Watch otters frolic and dolphins dance. And you won't want to miss our new Please Touch! exhibit—fun for children and adults of all ages!

ADMISSION

Adults	$5.00
Seniors and Students	$4.00
Children	$3.00
Children under 3	Free

HOURS

Sunday–Thursday:
10:00 A.M. to 5:00 P.M.
Friday and Saturday:
10:00 A.M. to 8:00 P.M.

WHAT'S GOING ON?

Daily Tours
See the Aquarium with our trained volunteer guides. Meet at the main entrance. Tours begin at 10:15, 11:15, 1:15, 2:15, 3:15.

Marine Life Films
Join us in the theater for exciting wildlife films. 1:00 and 3:00.

Feeding Times
Sea Lions 11:00, 2:00, 4:00
Penguins 10:30, 2:30

KEY

 Restrooms

 Telephone

 Restaurant

 Information

To Parking Area →

Wyeth Street

Gift Shop

Entrance

Brochures

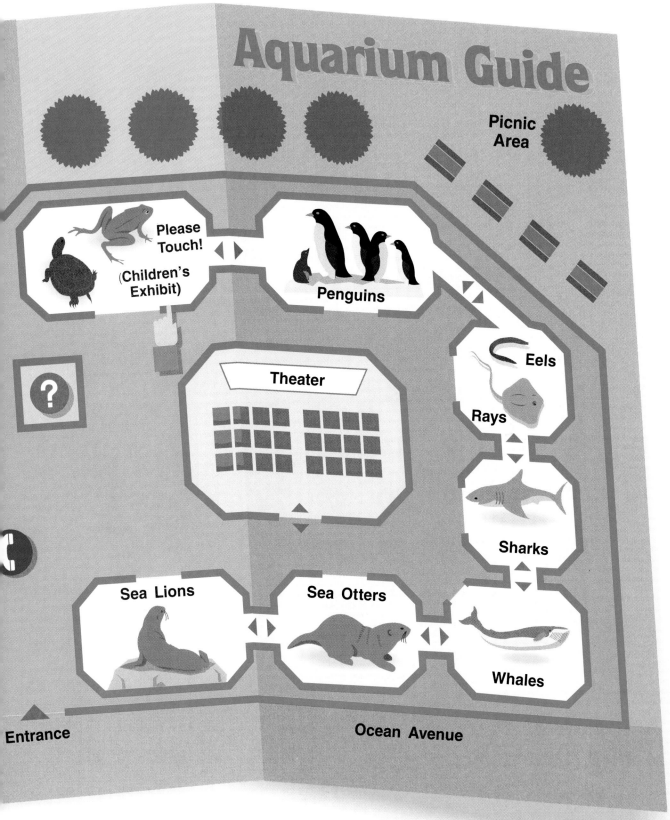

Calendar
▼▼▼▼▼▼▼▼

1997

JANUARY

SUN	MON	TUES	WED	THURS	FRI	SAT
			1	2	3	4
5	6	7	8	9	10	11
12	13	14	15	16	17	18
19	20	21	22	23	24	25
26	27	28	29	30	31	

FEBRUARY

SUN	MON	TUES	WED	THURS	FRI	SAT
						1
2	3	4	5	6	7	8
9	10	11	12	13	14	15
16	17	18	19	20	21	22
23	24	25	26	27	28	

MARCH

SUN	MON	TUES	WED	THURS	FRI	SAT
						1
2	3	4	5	6	7	8
9	10	11	12	13	14	15
16	17	18	19	20	21	22
23/30	24/31	25	26	27	28	29

APRIL

SUN	MON	TUES	WED	THURS	FRI	SAT
		1	2	3	4	5
6	7	8	9	10	11	12
13	14	15	16	17	18	19
20	21	22	23	24	25	26
27	28	29	30			

MAY

SUN	MON	TUES	WED	THURS	FRI	SAT
				1	2	3
4	5	6	7	8	9	10
11	12	13	14	15	16	17
18	19	20	21	22	23	24
25	26	27	28	29	30	31

JUNE

SUN	MON	TUES	WED	THURS	FRI	SAT
1	2	3	4	5	6	7
8	9	10	11	12	13	14
15	16	17	18	19	20	21
22	23	24	25	26	27	28
29	30					

JULY

SUN	MON	TUES	WED	THURS	FRI	SAT
		1	2	3	4	5
6	7	8	9	10	11	12
13	14	15	16	17	18	19
20	21	22	23	24	25	26
27	28	29	30	31		

AUGUST

SUN	MON	TUES	WED	THURS	FRI	SAT
					1	2
3	4	5	6	7	8	9
10	11	12	13	14	15	16
17	18	19	20	21	22	23
24/31	25	26	27	28	29	30

SEPTEMBER

SUN	MON	TUES	WED	THURS	FRI	SAT
	1	2	3	4	5	6
7	8	9	10	11	12	13
14	15	16	17	18	19	20
21	22	23	24	25	26	27
28	29	30				

OCTOBER

SUN	MON	TUES	WED	THURS	FRI	SAT
			1	2	3	4
5	6	7	8	9	10	11
12	13	14	15	16	17	18
19	20	21	22	23	24	25
26	27	28	29	30	31	

NOVEMBER

SUN	MON	TUES	WED	THURS	FRI	SAT
						1
2	3	4	5	6	7	8
9	10	11	12	13	14	15
16	17	18	19	20	21	22
23/30	24	25	26	27	28	29

DECEMBER

SUN	MON	TUES	WED	THURS	FRI	SAT
	1	2	3	4	5	6
7	8	9	10	11	12	13
14	15	16	17	18	19	20
21	22	23	24	25	26	27
28	29	30	31			

PRESIDENT'S DAY!
FEBRUARY 17th

Diagrams

Welcome to Leon's House

Attic

Marcia and Marlene's Room

Stairway

Bathroom

Mother's Room

Kitchen

Living Room

Leon's Room

Grandma's Room

Our Solar System

The nine planets of our solar system move around the Sun.

Pluto

Neptune

Uranus

Mars

Earth

Mercury

Venus

Sun

Saturn

Jupiter

Dictionary

Main
Entry

permit / pharmacy

permit
Permit means to allow someone to do something. My parents will not **permit** my sister and me to play outside after it is dark. ▲ **permitted, permitting.**

person

Definition

A **person** is a man, woman, or child. Fifty people can ride on the bus, but only one **person** can drive it. ▲ **persons.**

Illustration

Caption

The veterinarian will see many kinds of **pets** today.

pet
A **pet** is an animal that people care for in their homes. Dogs and cats are **pets.** Helen has two parakeets as **pets.** ▲ **pets.**

petal
A **petal** is a part of a flower. The **petals** of a daisy are narrow and white or yellow. ▲ **petals.**

pharmacy
A **pharmacy** is a store where drugs and medicines are sold. Another name for pharmacy is **drugstore.** ▲ **pharmacies.**

Plural

248

Dictionary

Guide Words

phone
1. **Phone** is a short word for **telephone.** The Colemans have three **phones** in their house. ▲ **phones.**
2. **Phone** means to use a telephone. We **phoned** my aunt tonight to sing "Happy Birthday" to her. ▲ **phoned, phoning.**

photograph
A **photograph** is a picture that you take with a camera. Polly took a **photograph** of our class. ▲ **photographs.**

piano
A **piano** is something that makes music. **Pianos** have black and white keys that you play with your fingers. Ian practices the **piano** every day for his concert. ▲ **pianos.**

pick
1. **Pick** means to take something in your hand. We're going to **pick** some flowers for Dad's birthday. The children **picked** up their toys and put them away.
2. **Pick** also means to choose something. Mom helped me **pick** a dress to wear to the party. ▲ **picked, picking.**

picnic
When you go on a **picnic,** you take food with you to eat outdoors. We brought sandwiches and fruit for a **picnic.** ▲ **picnics.**

picture
A **picture** is something that you draw or paint. You can also take **pictures** with a camera. I have a **picture** of a boat on my wall. ▲ **pictures.**

Renee is practicing a new song on the **piano.**

Photograph

Example Sentence

Verb Forms

Kim and Angela are **picking** flowers for their new neighbor.

Directions
▼▼▼▼▼▼▼▼▼▼

NATURAL DYEING

WHAT YOU WILL NEED:
- stove or hot plate
- large kettle
- water
- a white cotton garment (T-shirt, socks)
- various natural substances

NATURAL SUBSTANCES DYE CHART

marigold flowers		red onion skin	
sage		acorns	
walnut shells		berries	
tea		coffee	
spinach		dandelion roots	
yellow onion skin		beets	

Directions

▼▼▼▼▼▼▼▼▼▼▼

WHAT TO DO:

1. Fill the large kettle with water and put it on the stove or hot plate.

2. Turn on the heat.

3. Add the natural substance for the color you want.

4. Allow the water to simmer until it is darker than you want your garment to be.

5. Put the garment loosely into the water and simmer it until it is darker than you want it. (The garment will be lighter when it dries.)

6. Remove the garment from the kettle and rinse it in cold water.

7. Wring out the garment and hang it up to dry.

8. If you are not going to dye anything else, turn off the heat and empty the kettle.

Forms and Applications

Sunset Springs Library
Children's Room
Please Print

First Name: Sandra

Jackson
Last Name

24 Bonnett Avenue
Street Address

Sunset Springs
City

State: Arizona   Zip Code: 00000

Date of Birth: July 9, 1990

555-0354
Phone Number

Clinton Elementary
School

Grade: 2

First Name: Carl

Jackson
Parent or Guardian—Last Name

Please read the statement below and sign your name:
I will obey the rules of the Sunset Springs Library. I will
notify the library if I change my address or lose my card.

Sandra Jackson   10/10/97
Signature   *Date*

Please help us serve you better by answering the
questions below.

1. Do you enjoy reading in a language other than English?
   If so, name the language below.

   Language _____

2. When are you most likely to visit the library?
   (Check one or both choices.)
   ___ weekends   ✔ after school

Graphs

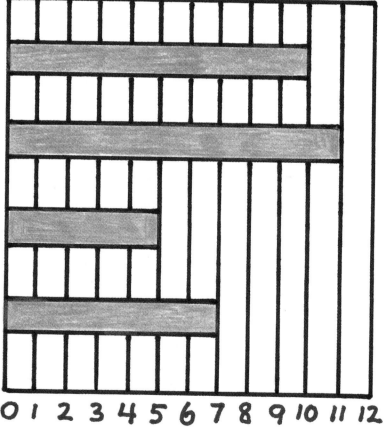

How We Get to School

By the Second Graders of Rooms 22 and 24

Ways of Traveling

Walk

Bus

Car

Bike

0 1 2 3 4 5 6 7 8 9 10 11 12

Number of Children

Maps

NEW
JERSEY

THE
BRONX

HUDSON RIVER

MANHATTAN

QUEENS

■ 1.
■ 2

GOVERNOR'S ISLAND

■ 3.
Buttermilk
Channel   Red Hook

BROOKLYN

UPPER
NEW YORK
BAY

The
Narrows

VERRAZANO-
NARROWS
BRIDGE

STATEN
ISLAND

LOWER
NEW YORK
BAY

A T L A N

Maps

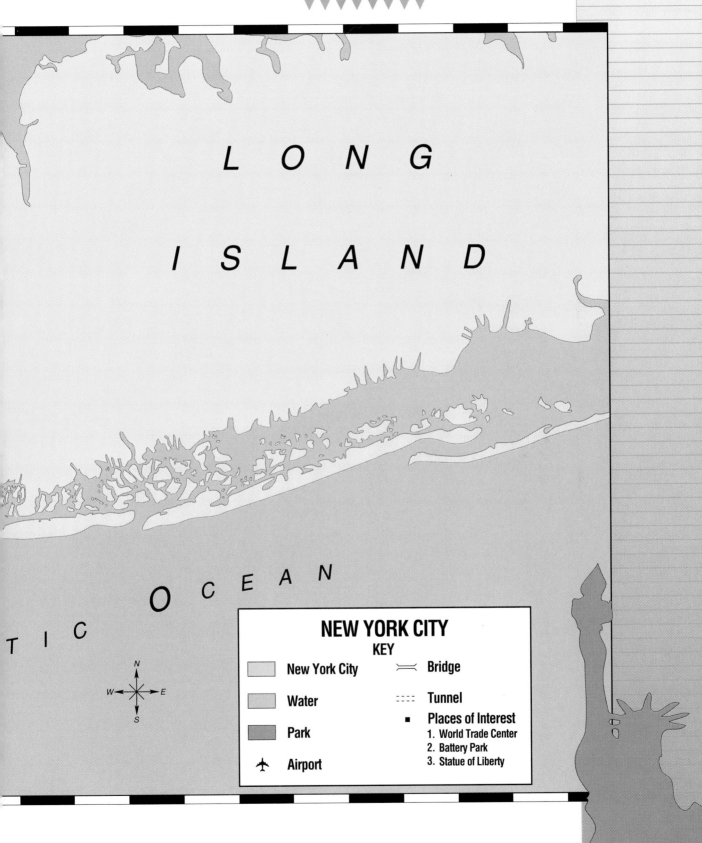

LONG ISLAND

ATLANTIC OCEAN

N
W — E
S

NEW YORK CITY
KEY

New York City   ⫤ Bridge

Water   ┅ Tunnel

Park   ■ Places of Interest
1. World Trade Center
2. Battery Park
3. Statue of Liberty

✈ Airport

Menus

Soups
Miso Soup 1.50
Clam Soup 1.50

Salads
House Salad 4.25
Seaweed Salad 5.00

Appetizers
Fish Cakes 4.50
Crab Cakes 5.50
Yakitori 5.50
   *Barbecued chicken
   on skewers*
Pipi Kaula 6.25
   Smoked beef
Laulau 6.25
   *Pork or chicken
   wrapped in taro leaves*

Entrees
Teriyaki 10.50
   *Beef, shrimp,
   or chicken broiled
   in teriyaki sauce*
Grilled Seafood 9.75
   *Ebi (Shrimp)
   Shutome (Swordfish)
   Opakapaka (Snapper)
   Ahi (Tuna)
   Tako (Squid)
   Mano (Shark)*
Kalua Pig 10.50
   Roast pig
Kalbi Ribs 10.50
Huli Huli Chicken . . . 9.75
   *Chicken seasoned
   in soy sauce*

Sushi

Sushi Special	11.00
Sashimi Special	11.00

Side Orders

Grilled Vegetables	4.50
Cooked Seaweed	4.50
Rice	1.75
Poi (Mashed taro root)	2.50

Desserts

Haupia (Coconut pudding)	2.50
Kulolo (Taro root pudding)	2.00
Chocolate Cake	2.50
Coconut Cake	2.50
Papaya Tart	3.25
Ice Cream	2.00
Fresh Fruit	2.00

Hawaiian Luau Dinner
$14.95
A delicious dinner, including:
Laulau
Pipikaula
Kalua Pig
Kalbi Ribs
Poi
****
Dessert
Salad
Beverage

GLOS

This glossary can help you to find out the meanings of words in this book that you may not know.

SARY

The words are listed in alphabetical order. Guide words at the top of each page tell you the first and last words on the page.

Aa

airplane

An **airplane** is a large vehicle that can fly. An **airplane** can carry people, packages, and other things from one place to another. ▲ **airplanes.**

airplane

almost

Almost means close to. It is **almost** 2 o'clock.

angry

When people are **angry** they are mad at someone or something. Mom was **angry** at the dog for chewing her slippers. ▲ **angrier, angriest.**

answer

An **answer** is the solution to a problem. Sue knew the **answer** to the math problem. ▲ **answered, answering.**

apartment

An **apartment** is a set of rooms to live in found in a large building. Sam lives in an **apartment** with his family. ▲ **apartments.**

asleep

When you are **asleep,** you are not awake. Nina had a funny dream while she was **asleep.**

asleep

awful

Awful means terrible or very bad. The medicine I had to take tasted **awful.**

Bb

beat

Beat means to hit something again and again. The rain **beat** against the window.
▲ **beaten, beating.**

become

To **become** means to grow to be something. Kittens grow older and **become** cats. ▲ **became, becoming.**

bedroom

A **bedroom** is a room that people use for sleeping. The sun came through my **bedroom** window.
▲ **bedrooms.**

between

Between means in the middle of two other things. In the alphabet, *s* comes **between** *r* and *t*.

beyond

Beyond means on the far side of. Our camp is just **beyond** those trees.

bottom

The **bottom** is the lowest part of something. The rock sank to the **bottom** of the pool. ▲ **bottoms.**

breath

Breath is the air you take in and let out when you breathe. When it is very cold, you can see your **breath.** ▲ **breaths.**

bridge

A **bridge** is something that is built across water. We drove over the **bridge.**
▲ **bridges.**

bridge

brush

Brush means to clean or make something neat using a light stroking movement. Jim likes to **brush** his dog at least once a week. ▲ **brushed, brushing.**

build

To **build** means to make something. They wanted to **build** a sandcastle at the beach. ▲ **built, building, builds.**

build

busy

When people are **busy,** they are doing something. Roberta can't come out to play because she is **busy** doing her homework. ▲ **busier, busiest.**

Cc

careful

If you are **careful,** you are thinking about what you are doing. Tina is very **careful** not to spill the paint.

carry

Carry means to hold something while moving it from one place to another. Mike will **carry** the groceries into the house for his mom. ▲ **carried, carrying.**

choose

Choose means to pick out something you want to have. Billy wanted to **choose** a gift for his grandmother. ▲ **chose, chosen, choosing.**

corner

A **corner** is a place where two lines or sides come together. Paul bumped his knee on the **corner** of the table. ▲ **corners.**

course

When you follow a **course,** you follow a certain way to get from one place to another. The airplane flew off its **course** because of the storm. ▲ **courses.**

curly

Curly means that something is in the shape of a little circle. Sally has **curly** hair. ▲ **curlier, curliest.**

Dd

decide

When you **decide** to do something, you choose to do one thing instead of another. Carlos may **decide** to have cereal instead of eggs. ▲ **decided, deciding.**

different

When something is **different,** it is not the same as something else. A duck is **different** from a goose.

different

downstairs

When you go **downstairs,** you go to a lower floor. I went **downstairs** to answer the door.

dream

A **dream** is a picture in your mind that you have when you are asleep. Last night Carol had a **dream** that she could fly. ▲ **dreams.**

duplicate

Duplicate means to make an exact copy of something or to do something again. We tried to **duplicate** last year's victory. ▲ **duplicated, duplicating.**

dye

To **dye** means to color or stain cloth, hair, food, or other materials. Robin's cousin wanted to **dye** his hair red. Another word that sounds like this is **die.** ▲ **dyes, dyeing.**

Ee

Earth

Earth is the planet we live on. It takes one year for **Earth** to go around the sun.

Earth

easy

When something is **easy,** it is not hard to do. The test was **easy.** ▲ **easier, easiest.**

either

Either is used when we talk about two of anything, and we mean one or the other. Rosie wanted **either** a ball or a kite.

escape

Escape means to get away from something. People knew that a hurricane was coming and were able to **escape** without getting hurt.
▲ **escaped, escaping.**

explain

When you **explain** something, you help another person understand it. Rosa will **explain** her poem to the class.
▲ **explained, explaining.**

finish

Finish means to get to the end of something. When I **finish** writing the letter, I will mail it.
▲ **finished, finishing.**

flop

To move around or flap loosely. The dog's ears **flop** when it runs.
▲ **flopped, flopping.**

forest

A **forest** is a large area of land covered by trees and other plants. They went camping in the **forest.**
▲ **forests.**

forest

forever

Forever means something that will never end. The boy and girl in the fairy tale wanted to stay young **forever.**

forget

Forget means to not remember something. Josie was afraid she would **forget** my address, so she wrote it down. ▲ **forgot, forgetting.**

Gg

garden

A **garden** is a place where people grow flowers or vegetables. When our cousins visit, they always bring us fresh tomatoes from their **garden.** ▲ **gardens.**

garden

giant

1. **Giant** means very big. Many of the dinosaurs that lived millions of years ago were **giant** animals.
2. A **giant** is also a huge make-believe person. The **giant** in the story could hold three people in one hand. ▲ **giants.**

giant

giggle

When you **giggle** you laugh in a silly way. We began to **giggle** when my little brother put his socks on his ears. ▲ **giggled, giggling.**

grab

Grab means to take hold of suddenly. The baby tried to **grab** my hair. ▲ **grabbed, grabbing.**

grandmother

Your **grandmother** is your father's mother or your mother's mother. Sometimes a **grandmother** is called grandma or nana. My **grandmother** lives in New York City. ▲ **grandmothers.**

growl

Growl means to make a deep, angry sound in the throat. The dogs **growl** when someone knocks on the door. ▲ **growled, growling.**

Hh

happen

Happen means to take place. If you listen to the story, you will hear what **happens** next. ▲ **happened, happening.**

harbor

A **harbor** is a safe place for boats near the shore in either lakes, rivers, or oceans. We watched the fishing boats come into the **harbor.** ▲ **harbors.**

harbor

hide

Hide means to put yourself or something else in a place where it cannot be seen. My cat likes to **hide** under my bed. ▲ **hid, hidden,** or **hid, hiding.**

Ii

important

When something is **important,** it means that you should pay attention to it. It is **important** that you look both ways before you cross the street.

island

An **island** is land that has water all around it. My aunt lives on an **island,** so we have to take a boat to visit her. ▲ **islands.**

Kk

kitchen

A **kitchen** is a room where people cook and serve food. Martin's family eats in the **kitchen.** ▲ **kitchens.**

Ll

large

Large means big. Elephants and whales are **large** animals. ▲ **larger, largest.**

lei

A **lei** is a chain made of flowers often worn in Hawaii. When Kate went to visit her aunt in Hawaii she was given a beautiful **lei.** Another word that sounds like this is **lay.** ▲ **leis.**

lei

linen

Linen is a strong cloth made from the flax plant used to make clothing, tablecloths, and sheets. My aunt was busy folding the **linen** napkins.

lonely

1. When you feel **lonely,** you feel unhappy about being by yourself. Gabe is **lonely** because all his friends are away for the summer. **2.** Something that is away from others. A **lonely** tree grew in the field. ▲ **lonelier, loneliest.**

loud

Something that is **loud** makes a lot of noise. The alarm clock made a **loud** buzzing noise. ▲ **louder, loudest.**

middle

The **middle** is a place halfway between two points or sides. Noon is in the **middle** of the day. ▲ **middles.**

Nn

nature

Nature means all things in the world that are not made by people. Plants, animals, mountains, and oceans are all part of **nature.**

notice

1. When you **notice** something, you see it or pay attention to it. In the autumn, Erin began to **notice** that the days seemed to be getting shorter and the nights seemed to be getting longer. ▲ **noticed, noticing.**
2. A **notice** also means a printed message to make something known. Benji got a **notice** that the circus was coming to town next week. ▲ **notices.**

Oo

ocean

An **ocean** is a body of salt water and covers large areas of the earth. Fish and whales live in the **ocean.** ▲ **oceans.**

often

When something happens **often** it happens many times over and over again. Kate **often** eats cereal for breakfast.

Pp

pajamas

Pajamas are a shirt and a pair of pants that you wear when you go to bed. Jessica's favorite **pajamas** have red polka dots.

planet

A **planet** is any one of the nine large bodies that revolve around the sun, including Earth. The spaceship landed on the **planet** Mars. ▲ **planets.**

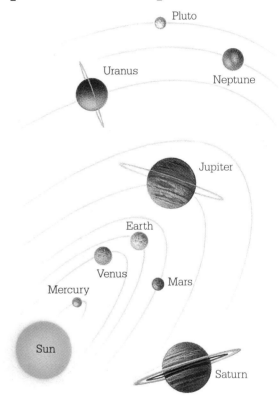

Pluto

Uranus

Neptune

Jupiter

Earth

Venus

Mars

Mercury

Sun

Saturn

planets

practice

Practice means doing something over and over until you do it well. I will **practice** riding my bike after school. ▲ **practiced, practicing.**

pretend

Pretend means to make believe. Tomás and Janie often **pretend** to be robots. ▲ **pretended, pretending.**

pull

When you **pull** something, you move it toward you. I tried to **pull** the door open. ▲ **pulled, pulling.**

purr

Purr means to make a soft, quiet sound. Cats **purr** when they are happy. ▲ **purred, purring.**

Qq

quick

When something is **quick,** it means that it moves fast or happens in a short time. We ate a **quick** lunch. ▲ **quicker, quickest.**

quilt

A **quilt** is like a blanket. I sleep under a soft, warm **quilt** during the winter. ▲ **quilts.**

Rr

rainbow

The bright colors you sometimes see in the sky after it rains are called a **rainbow.** The **rainbow** appeared after the thunderstorm. ▲ **rainbows.**

rainbow

rattle

To **rattle** means to make a lot of short, sharp sounds by shaking or hitting something. The windows **rattle** when the wind blows during a storm. ▲ **rattled, rattling.**

rush

Rush means to move, go, or come quickly. We have to **rush** or we'll miss the bus and be late for school. ▲ **rushed, rushing.**

Ss

safe

Safe means to be protected from danger. William put his favorite book on the shelf where it would be **safe.** ▲ **safer, safest.**

scare

If something **scares** you, it makes you feel afraid. Loud noises always **scare** the puppy. ▲ **scared, scaring.**

shell

A **shell** is a hard outer covering that protects something. A turtle has a hard **shell** on its back. ▲ **shells.**

shell

shine

Shine means to give out light or to be bright. The sun **shines** during the day. ▲ **shone** or **shined, shining.**

short

Short means not far from one end to another. My dog has **short** legs.
▲ **shorter, shortest.**

signal

To **signal** is to show people what to do without using words. The children waited for the crossing guard to **signal** them to cross the street. ▲ **signals.**

signal

smart

A person who is **smart** is clever or bright. Leah is a **smart** girl who does well in school. ▲ **smarter, smartest.**

soft

When a sound is **soft**, it is gentle and quiet. Since the baby was sleeping, the mother spoke in a very **soft** voice.

space

1. Space is a place that has nothing in it. Write your name in the **space** on the paper. ▲ **spaces.**
2. Space is also the place where all of the planets and stars are found. The earth, moon, and sun are in **space.**

spin

Spin means to go around in a circle. Chuck loves to **spin** his toy top. ▲ **spun, spinning.**

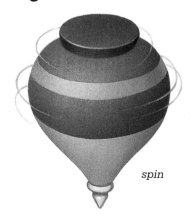

spin

G15

storm

During a **storm,** it rains or snows and the wind blows hard. I wore my raincoat during the **storm.** ▲ **storms.**

storm

straight

If something is **straight,** it does not bend. I used a ruler to draw a **straight** line on the paper.

▲ **straighter, straightest.**

stripe

A **stripe** is a long line that is a different color from what is next to it. Sally wore a blue shirt with a green **stripe** to the party. ▲ **stripes.**

strong

If something is **strong,** it means that it has a lot of power. The wind was so **strong** that it blew down a big tree. ▲ **stronger, strongest.**

sudden

When something is **sudden,** it means it happens very fast. There was a **sudden** storm. ▲ **suddenly.**

sunlight

Sunlight is the light from the sun. Plants, animals, and humans all need **sunlight** to grow and to be healthy.

Tt

through

1. Through means from one side or end to the other. The children crawled **through** the tunnel in the playground.
2. Through also means finished. I will be **through** with my homework soon.

treasure

A **treasure** is money, jewelry, or other things that are of great value. The king and queen hid their **treasure** in a special room. ▲ **treasures.**

treasure

twig

A **twig** is a tiny branch of a tree. After climbing the tree, I found a **twig** in my hair. ▲ **twigs.**

Uu

upstairs

When you go **upstairs,** you go to a higher floor. My brother's bedroom is downstairs, but my bedroom is **upstairs.**

Ww

whale

A **whale** is a very large animal that lives in the ocean. I saw a blue **whale** at the aquarium.
▲ **whales.**

wild

To be **wild** means that something is not controlled by people and lives naturally. There are **wild** horses living on that island. ▲ **wilder, wildest.**

wonderful

Wonderful means amazing, unusual, or very good. At the circus we all stared at the **wonderful** acrobats.

wool

Wool is a kind of cloth that is made from the hair of a sheep or other animals. **Wool** is used to make sweaters, mittens, coats, and blankets.

wool

worry

When you **worry** it means that you feel a little afraid about something. Mom and Dad start to **worry** if we come home late from school. ▲ **worried, worrying.**

wrap

Wrap means to cover something by putting something else around it. We will **wrap** a blanket around us to keep warm. ▲ **wrapped, wrapping.**

yarn

Yarn is thread spun from fiber that has been twisted into long strands. Amy's grandmother is making each of her grandchildren a sweater out of **yarn.**

ACKNOWLEDGMENTS

The publisher gratefully acknowledges permission to reprint the following copyrighted material:

"Adopting Daisy," art by Mike Eagle, from LADYBUG, THE MAGAZINE FOR YOUNG CHILDREN, October 1993 issue, Copyright © 1993, Carus Publishing Company. Reprinted by permission.

"Andre" by Gwendolyn Brooks. Reprinted by permission.

Cover illustration of CAN I KEEP HIM? by Steven Kellogg. Copyright © 1971 by Steven Kellogg. Used by permission of Dial Books for Young Readers, a division of Penguin Books USA Inc.

"Carry Go Bring Come" from CARRY GO BRING COME by Vyanne Samuels. Text copyright (c) 1988 by Vyanne Samuels. Illustrations copyright (c) 1988 by Jennifer Northway. Reprinted with permission of Simon & Schuster Books for Young Readers, Simon & Schuster Children's Publishing Division.

"Charlie Anderson" by Barbara Abercrombie, illustrated by Mark Graham, Text copyright (c) 1990 by Barbara Abercrombie. Illustrations copyright (c) 1990 by Mark Graham. Reprinted with permission of Margaret K. McElderry Books, Simon & Schuster Children's Publishing Division.

"Everybody Says" by Dorothy Aldis reprinted by permission of G.P. Putnam & Sons from EVERYTHING AND ANYTHING, copyright © 1925-1927, © renewed 1953-1955 by Dorothy Aldis.

Cover of FLY AWAY HOME by Eve Bunting. Jacket copyright (c) 1991 by Ronald Himler. Reprinted by permission of Clarion Books-Houghton Mifflin Co. All rights reserved.

"The Goat in the Rug" from THE GOAT IN THE RUG by Charles Blood and Martin A. Link. Copyright © 1980 by Charles L. Blood and Martin A. Link. Illustrations copyright © 1980 by Nancy Winslow Parker. Reprinted with the permission of Simon & Schuster Books For Young Readers.

Cover reprinted with the permission of Simon & Schuster Books for Young Readers from HENRY AND MUDGE AND THE FOREVER SEA by Cynthia Rylant, illustrated by Suçie Stevenson. Illustration copyright (c) 1989 Suçie Stevenson.

"Henry's Wrong Turn" from HENRY'S WRONG TURN by Harriet Ziefert. Text Copyright © 1989 by Harriet Ziefert; Illustrations Copyright © 1989 by Andrea Baruffi. By permission of Little, Brown and Company.

"Hey, Bug!" by Lilian Moore. Reprinted by permission.

"Hugs and Kisses" from THE SUN IS ON by Lindamichellebaron. Reprinted by permission of Harlin Jacque Publications.

Cover from THE ISLAND OF THE SKOG by Steven Kellogg. Copyright © 1973 by Steven Kellogg. Used by permission of Dial Books for Young Readers, a division of Penguin Books USA Inc.

"Lei Day: Party in the Islands!" reprinted from OWL magazine with permission of the publisher, Owl Communications Inc., Toronto, Canada.

"The Light-House-Keeper's White-Mouse" from YOU READ TO ME, I'LL READ TO YOU by John Ciardi. Copyright © 1962 by John Ciardi. Copyright © 1990 renewed. Reprinted by permission of the Ciardi Family.

"Looking Around" by Aileen Fisher. By permission of the author, who controls the rights.

"Lost" from FAR AND FEW by David McCord. Copyright by David McCord © 1952 by David McCord. By permission Little, Brown and Company.

"Luka's Quilt" by Georgia Guback. Copyright © 1994 by Georgia Guback, published by Greenwillow Books. Reprinted by permission.

"My Horse, Fly Like a Bird" Copyright © 1989 by Virginia Driving Hawk Sneve. All rights reserved. Reprinted from DANCING TEPEES: POEMS OF AMERICAN INDIAN YOUTH by permission of Holiday House.

"The Mysterious Tadpole" from THE MYSTERIOUS TADPOLE by Steven Kellogg. Copyright © by Steven Kellogg. Used by permission of Dial Books for Young Readers, a division of Penguin Books USA Inc.

"Nine-in-One, Grr! Grr!" by Blia Xiong reprinted with permission of Children's Book Press, San Francisco, CA.

"October Saturday" by Bobbie Katz. Copyright © 1990 by Bobbie Katz. Used by permission of Bobbie Katz, who controls all rights.

The book cover of PATRICK'S DINOSAURS by Carol Carrick, illustrated by Donald Carrick, Copyright © 1983, published by Clarion Books of Houghton Mifflin, is reprinted by permission of the publisher.

"The Puppy and I" from WHEN WE WERE VERY YOUNG by A. A. Milne. Illustrations by E. H. Shepard. Copyright © 1924 by E. P. Dutton, renewed 1952 by A. A. Milne. Used by permission of Dutton's Children's Books, a division of Penguin Books USA Inc.

"Relatives" from THE BUTTERFLY JAR by Jeff Moss. Copyright © 1989 by Jeff Moss. Used by permission of Bantam Books, a division of Bantam Doubleday Dell Publishing Group, Inc.

The book cover of SLEEP OUT by Carol Carrick, illustrated by Donald Carrick. Copyright © 1979, published by Clarion Books of Houghton Mifflin, is reprinted by permission of the publisher.

"A Spike of Green" by Barbara Baker. Reprinted by permission.

"The Sun Is Always Shining Somewhere" by Allan Fowler, Copyright © 1991 by Children's Press, Inc., published by Children's Press. Reprinted by permission.

"Swimmy" from SWIMMY by Leo Lionni. Copyright © 1963 by Leo Lionni. Reprinted by permission of Pantheon Books, a division of Random House, Inc.

"Tigers" from YOUR BIG BACKYARD Series 1, Number 5, May 1995 issue, copyright © 1980, published by the National Wildlife Federation. Reprinted by permission.

The book cover of THE WALL by Eve Bunting, illustrated by Ronald Himler, Copyright © 1990, published by Houghton Mifflin, is reprinted by permission of the publisher.

"The Wednesday Surprise" from THE WEDNESDAY SURPRISE by Eve Bunting with illustrations by Donald Carrick. Text copyright © 1989 by Eve Bunting. Illustrations copyright © 1989 by Donald Carrick. Reprinted by permission of Clarion Books, a Houghton Mifflin Co. imprint.

"What in the World?" from THERE IS NO RHYME FOR SILVER by Eve Merriam. Copyright © 1962 by Eve Merriam. Copyright renewed by Eve Merriam. Reprinted by permission of Marian Reiner for author.

"What Is a Shadow?" by Bob Ridiman, Illustration by True Kelley, from LADYBUG magazine for young children July 1993 issue, copyright © 1993, published by Carus Publishing Company. Reprinted by permission.

"Willie's Not the Hugging Kind" is the entire work from WILLIE'S NOT THE HUGGING KIND by Joyce Durham Barrett, illustrated by Pat Cummings. Text copyright © 1989 by Joyce Durham Barrett. Illustrations copyright © 1989 by Pat Cummings. Reprinted by permission of Harper/Collins Publishers.

"A Wool Surprise for Kenji" by Sue Katharine Jackson, illustrated by Dora Leder, from LADYBUG magazine for young children January 1994 issue, Copyright © 1994, published by Carus Publishing Company. Reprinted by permission.

READING RESOURCES

Book Parts: Excerpt reprinted with the permission of Simon & Schuster Books For Young Readers. from HENRY AND MUDGE AND THE BEDTIME THUMPS by Cynthia Rylant, illustrated by Suçie Stevenson. Text, copyright © 1991 by Cynthia Rylant. Illustration, copyright © by Suçie Stevenson.

Dictionary: Excerpt from MACMILLAN PRIMARY DICTIONARY. copyright © 1991 by Macmillan/McGraw-Hill School Publishing Company. Reprinted by permission of Macmillan/McGraw-Hill School Publishing Company.

COVER DESIGN: Carbone Smolan Associates
COVER ILLUSTRATION: Alex Schaefer (front - bears), Floyd Cooper (front - horseshoes), Consuelo Udave (back)

DESIGN CREDITS
Carbone Smolan Associates, front matter and unit openers
Bill Smith Studio, 54-57, 92-93, 144-147, 200-203, 292-295
Function Thru Form, Inc., 344-345, 348-353, 358-359, 362-363
Sheldon Cotler + Associates Editorial Group, 40-53, 58-59, 94-119
Notovitz Design Inc., 346-347, 354-357, 360-361

ILLUSTRATION CREDITS
Unit 1: Alex Schaefer, 10-11; Mary Collier, 38-39; K. W. Popp, 60-61 (bkgd.); Jerry Pavey, 62-91 (typography and bkgds.); William Neeper, 92-93 (title); Jada Rowland, 117; Sennelli Ortiz, 118-119. **Unit 2:** Consuelo Udave, 120-121; Margaret Cusak, 176-177; Dale Verzaal, 204-205; Catherine O'Neill, 232-233. **Unit 3:** Floyd Cooper, 234-235; Carol Schwartz, 236-237; Margaret Cusack, 292 (title); Krista Brauckmann-Towns, 298-299; John Steven Gurney, 324-325; Loretta Krupinski, 342-343. **Reading Resources:** Randy Chewning, 346-347, 354-355; Bob Mansfield, 348-349; Patrick Merrill, 352; Maria Lauricella, 353; Alex Bloch, 356-357; Paul Meisel, 358; Felicia Telsey, 359; Graphic Chart and Map Co., 360-361; Denny Bond, 362-363. **Glossary:** Will and Cory Nelson, G2, G5, G8, G10, G12, G14, G15, G17; Bob Pepper, G4.

PHOTOGRAPHY CREDITS
All photographs are by the Macmillan/McGraw-Hill School Division (MMSD) except as noted below;

37: b. Mark Graham; t. Barbara Abercrombie. 58-59: Arie de Zanger for MMSD. 62-91: Ann Oliver/American Quilters Society. **Unit 2** 122-143: John Cancalosi/Valan Photos. 123: Phil Norton/Valan Photos. 124: David Young Wolf/PhotoEdit. 125: John Fowler/Valan Photos. 126: Fernando Diez/The Image Bank. 127: Phil Norton/Valan Photos. 128: Val Whelan/Valan Photos. 129: V. Whelan/Valan Photos. 131: Stephen Krasemann/Valan Photos. 133: Kennon Cooke/Valan Photos. 135: t. J.A. Wilkinson/Valan Photos; b. V.Wilkinson/Valan Photos. 137: